Media Ethics

Other Books in the Current Controversies Series

Media Ethics

Noël Merino, Book Editor

GREENHAVEN PRESS
A part of Gale, Cengage Learning

GALE
CENGAGE Learning·

Detroit • New York • San Francisco • New Haven, Conn • Waterville, Maine • London

Elizabeth Des Chenes, *Director, Publishing Solutions*

© 2013 Greenhaven Press, a part of Gale, Cengage Learning

Gale and Greenhaven Press are registered trademarks used herein under license.

For more information, contact:
Greenhaven Press
27500 Drake Rd.
Farmington Hills, MI 48331-3535
Or you can visit our Internet site at gale.cengage.com

For product information and technology assistance, contact us at

Gale Customer Support, 1-800-877-4253
For permission to use material from this text or product, submit all requests online at
www.cengage.com/permissions

Further permissions questions can be emailed to permissionrequest@cengage.com

Articles in Greenhaven Press anthologies are often edited for length to meet page requirements. In addition, original titles of these works are changed to clearly present the main thesis and to explicitly indicate the author's opinion. Every effort is made to ensure that Greenhaven Press accurately reflects the original intent of the authors. Every effort has been made to trace the owners of copyrighted material.

Cover image copyright © IvicaNS/Shutterstock.com.

LIBRARY OF CONGRESS CATALOGING-IN-PUBLICATION DATA

Media ethics / Noël Merino, book editor.
     p. cm. -- (Current controversies)
     Includes bibliographical references and index.
     ISBN 978-0-7377-6237-2 (hardcover) -- ISBN 978-0-7377-6238-9 (pbk.)
     1. Journalistic ethics. I. Merino, Noël.
     PN4756.M353 2012
     174'.907--dc23
                                          2012017726

Printed in the United States of America
1 2 3 4 5 6 7 16 15 14 13 12

Contents

Chapter 1: What Is the Current State of Media Ethics?

Chapter 2: Should Telling the Truth Take Precedence over Other Ethical Concerns?

The use of deception in reporting undermines the respectability of journalism and should only be used when
absolutely necessary.

Chapter 3: Should Journalists Avoid Actions That Compromise Objectivity?

Yes: Journalists Should Avoid Actions That Compromise Objectivity

To avoid conflicts of interest, reporters should publicly disclose any large payments they receive for engagements outside their regular job.

No: Journalists Do Not Need to Avoid Actions That Compromise Objectivity

Chapter 4: How Have New Technologies Affected Media Ethics?

From the digital recorder to the laptop computer connected wirelessly to the Internet, technology has profoundly changed the way news is reported and distributed to users around the world.

Foreword

By definition, controversies are "discussions of questions in which opposing opinions clash" (Webster's Twentieth Century Dictionary Unabridged). Few would deny that controversies are a pervasive part of the human condition and exist on virtually every level of human enterprise. Controversies transpire between individuals and among groups, within nations and between nations. Controversies supply the grist necessary for progress by providing challenges and challengers to the status quo. They also create atmospheres where strife and warfare can flourish. A world without controversies would be a peaceful world; but it also would be, by and large, static and prosaic.

The Series' Purpose

The purpose of the Current Controversies series is to explore many of the social, political, and economic controversies dominating the national and international scenes today. Titles selected for inclusion in the series are highly focused and specific. For example, from the larger category of criminal justice, Current Controversies deals with specific topics such as police brutality, gun control, white collar crime, and others. The debates in Current Controversies also are presented in a useful, timeless fashion. Articles and book excerpts included in each title are selected if they contribute valuable, long-range ideas to the overall debate. And wherever possible, current information is enhanced with historical documents and other relevant materials. Thus, while individual titles are current in focus, every effort is made to ensure that they will not become quickly outdated. Books in the Current Controversies series will remain important resources for librarians, teachers, and students for many years.

In addition to keeping the titles focused and specific, great care is taken in the editorial format of each book in the series. Book introductions and chapter prefaces are offered to provide background material for readers. Chapters are organized around several key questions that are answered with diverse opinions representing all points on the political spectrum. Materials in each chapter include opinions in which authors clearly disagree as well as alternative opinions in which authors may agree on a broader issue but disagree on the possible solutions. In this way, the content of each volume in Current Controversies mirrors the mosaic of opinions encountered in society. Readers will quickly realize that there are many viable answers to these complex issues. By questioning each author's conclusions, students and casual readers can begin to develop the critical thinking skills so important to evaluating opinionated material.

Current Controversies is also ideal for controlled research. Each anthology in the series is composed of primary sources taken from a wide gamut of informational categories, including periodicals, newspapers, books, US and foreign government documents, and the publications of private and public organizations. Readers will find factual support for reports, debates, and research papers covering all areas of important issues. In addition, an annotated table of contents, an index, a book and periodical bibliography, and a list of organizations to contact are included in each book to expedite further research.

Perhaps more than ever before in history, people are confronted with diverse and contradictory information. During the Persian Gulf War, for example, the public was not only treated to minute-to-minute coverage of the war, it was also inundated with critiques of the coverage and countless analyses of the factors motivating US involvement. Being able to sort through the plethora of opinions accompanying today's major issues, and to draw one's own conclusions, can be a complicated and frustrating struggle. It is the editors' hope that Current Controversies will help readers with this struggle.

Introduction

> "*In the wake of the* News of the World *scandal is the question of whether their universally maligned tactics were an anomaly in the world of journalism or just the tip of the iceberg.*"

The British tabloid newspaper *News of the World* closed in July 2011 after 168 years of circulation, after a scandal involving evidence of extensive phone hacking. *News of the World* had long been known for engaging in questionable undercover reporting tactics. As early as 2005, there were allegations that the publication was hacking into the voicemail of members of the British Royal Family; and in 2006 the paper's royal editor and a private investigator were arrested over such allegations, both receiving prison sentences after admitting to hacking into the mobile phones of aides of the Royal Family. The phone hacking of celebrities and politicians continued, but public outrage reached a fever pitch in 2011 when evidence showed that the tabloid had hacked into the phone of a missing thirteen-year-old girl.

Milly Dowler went missing in March 2002. A nationwide search followed her disappearance, reported widely in the news. Her body was found almost six months later, and in June 2011 her murderer was sentenced to life in prison. A month later a lawyer for Dowler's parents said he learned from police that *News of the World* had hacked into Milly's phone a couple days after she disappeared and that some of her messages had been deleted to make room for more messages, causing police and Milly's family to believe she may still be alive. Although the tabloid admitted hacking into the missing girl's mobile phone, evidence has never confirmed whether *News of the World* deleted messages. The paper settled a lawsuit with the Dowlers in 2011.

During the several-year investigation of *News of the World*, it came to light that there were thousands of victims of phone hacking. Many celebrities and politicians settled lawsuits with the tabloid, including actress Sienna Miller, singer Charlotte Church, and comedian Steve Coogan. In addition, family members of other murdered victims also discovered phone hacking by *News of the World* and settled cases in the courts. It became clear that *News of the World* had a long history of using phone hacking as a way of getting news stories and a general lack of ethics in the organization, which ultimately led to its demise.

In the wake of the *News of the World* scandal is the question of whether their universally maligned tactics were an anomaly in the world of journalism or just the tip of the iceberg. *News of the World* was a Sunday sister paper to *The Sun*, still in publication, under the umbrella News International, which also publishes *The Times* and *The Sunday Times*. News International is part of the multinational media conglomerate News Corporation, whose chairman and chief executive is Rupert Murdoch. Notable media holdings in the United States include Fox News, the *Wall Street Journal*, and the *New York Post*.

Some have commented that all of Murdoch's publications—an extensive list—are suspect after the *News of the World* scandal. Carl Bernstein, the journalist who shared a Pulitzer Prize with Bob Woodward for his coverage of Watergate for *The Washington Post*, opines:

> As anyone in the business will tell you, the standards and culture of a journalistic institution are set from the top down, by its owner, publisher, and top editors. Reporters and editors do not routinely break the law, bribe policemen, wiretap, and generally conduct themselves like thugs unless it is a matter of recognized and understood policy. Private detectives and phone hackers do not become the primary sources of a newspaper's information without the tacit

knowledge and approval of the people at the top, all the more so in the case of newspapers owned by Rupert Murdoch, according to those who know him best.

Bernstein quotes a former top executive who said of the *News of the World* scandal, "Murdoch invented and established this culture in the newsroom, where you do whatever it takes to get the story, take no prisoners, destroy the competition, and the end will justify the means."[1]

In February 2012, News International began publication of *The Sun on Sunday*, a paper that essentially replaces *News of the World*. In an editorial in its first edition on February 26, it vowed:

> As we launch the seven day *Sun*, we want to strengthen that connection (with the readers) with a new independent *Sun* Readers' Champion to accept feedback and correct significant errors. Our journalists must abide by the Press Complaints Commission's editors code, the industry standard for ethical behaviour, and the News Corporation standards of business conduct.

Whether this vow will actually result in a departure from the culture of *News of the World* remains to be seen.

The *News of the World* scandal has brought to light many concerns about the current state of media ethics. What is at stake in the public's trust of the media? Are the news stories in the media gained by the use of unethical tactics? Does the public care if the stories are true? These debates and others are explored in *Current Controversies: Media Ethics*.

Notes

1. Carl Bernstein, "Murdoch's Watergate?" *Newsweek*, July 9, 2011.

CHAPTER 1

What is the Current State of Media Ethics?

Overview: Americans Have Mixed Views of the News Media

Pew Research Center for the People and the Press

The Pew Research Center for the People and the Press is an independent, nonpartisan public opinion research organization that studies attitudes toward politics, the press, and public policy issues.

Negative opinions about the performance of news organizations now equal or surpass all-time highs on nine of 12 core measures the Pew Research Center has been tracking since 1985. However, these bleak findings are put into some perspective by the fact that news organizations are more trusted sources of information than are many other institutions, including government and business.

Further, people rate the performance of the news organizations they rely on much more positively than they rate the performance of news organizations generally.

And the public's impressions of the national media may be influenced more by their opinions of cable news outlets than their views of other news sources, such as network or local TV news, newspapers or internet news outlets. When asked what first comes to mind when they think of "news organizations," most name a cable news outlet, with CNN and Fox News receiving the most mentions by far.

Americans' Views of Press Performance

The Pew Research Center for the People & the Press has been tracking views of press performance since 1985, and the overall ratings remain quite negative. Fully 66% say news stories often are inaccurate, 77% think that news organizations tend to favor one side, and 80% say news organizations are often influenced by powerful people and organizations.

The widely-shared belief that news stories are inaccurate cuts to the press's core mission: Just 25% say that in general news organizations get the facts straight while 66% say stories are often inaccurate. As recently as four years ago [2007], 39% said news organizations mostly get the facts straight and 53% said stories are often inaccurate.

But Americans have a very different view of the news sources they rely on than they do of the news media generally. When asked to rate the accuracy of stories from the sources where they get most of their news, the percentage saying these outlets get the facts straight more than doubles. Fully 62% say their main news sources get the facts straight, while just 30% say stories are often inaccurate.

Overall, television continues to be the public's main source for national and international news.

The biennial news attitudes survey was conducted July 20–24 [2011] among 1,501 adults nationwide, with supplemental data collected on other, smaller surveys in June, July and August. These surveys find that while the public holds news organizations in low regard, they are more trusted as a source of information than are federal, state and local governments, the [Barack] Obama administration and business corporations.

Nearly seven-in-ten (69%) say they have a lot or some trust in information they get from local news organizations, while 59% say they trust information from national news organizations.

By comparison, about half say they have a lot or some trust in information provided by their state government (51%) and the Obama administration (50%). Smaller percentages trust information from federal agencies (44%), business corporations (41%), Congress (37%) or candidates running for office (29%).

The Public's Main Source of News

Overall, television continues to be the public's main source for national and international news. Currently, 66% say they get most of their news from television, while 43% cite the internet as their main news source.[1] While this is little changed from last year, over the long term the gap between TV and the internet has narrowed: Four years ago, roughly three times as many people cited TV than the internet as their main source of national and international news (74% vs. 24%).

Despite the growth of internet news, it is clear that television news outlets, specifically cable news outlets, are central to people's impressions of the news media. When asked what first comes to mind when they think of news organizations, 63% volunteer the name of a cable news outlet, with CNN and Fox News by far the most prevalent in people's minds. Only about a third (36%) name one of the broadcast networks. Fewer than one-in-five mention local news outlets and only 5% mention a national newspaper such as the *New York Times, Wall Street Journal* or *USA Today*. Just 3% name a website—either web-only or linked to a traditional news organization—when asked what comes to mind when they think of news organizations.

A Growth in Negative Attitudes

The survey finds that the growth in negative attitudes toward the news media in recent years in several key areas has come among Democrats and independents. Since Barack Obama took office, the proportion of Democrats saying that news sto-

---

1. Survey percentages may not add up to 100% because multiple responses were permitted.

ries are often inaccurate has risen sharply, and they are now nearly as critical as Republicans.

In 2007, 43% of Democrats and 56% of independents said stories were often inaccurate. Since then, the percentage of Democrats expressing skepticism about the accuracy of news reports has increased by 21 points to 64%, and the percentage of independents saying this has grown by 10 points. Republican views have held fairly steady: 69% see stories as often inaccurate, little changed from four years ago (63%).

While the press's overall reputation in many areas has declined, majorities continue to say that news organizations care about how good a job they do (62%) and are highly professional (57%). However, these evaluations also have slipped somewhat since 2007.

Most Americans prefer news with no political point of view, and this feeling is particularly widespread when it comes to getting news online.

The public also continues to view press criticism of political leaders as a check on possible wrongdoing. A majority (58%) says "such criticism is worth it because it keeps political leaders from doing things that should not be done." Just a quarter (25%) say that press criticism of political leaders keeps them "from doing their job."

Partisan differences in views of the press's watchdog role have disappeared in recent years. In 2007, during the [George W.] Bush administration, 71% of Democrats and just 44% of Republicans said press criticism of political leaders was worth it because it kept them from doing things that should not be done. In 2009, after Obama took office, somewhat more Republicans (65%) than Democrats (55%) favored a watchdog role for the press. In the new survey, nearly identical percentages of Republicans (59%), Democrats (58%) and independents (58%) support the watchdog role.

Sources of News Online

The survey finds that most Americans prefer news with no political point of view, and this feeling is particularly widespread when it comes to getting news online. Fully 74% of online news consumers say they prefer internet sources that do not have a political point of view. Just 19% prefer sources that have a political point of view.

While the public has long been critical of many aspects of the press's performance, negative attitudes are at record levels in a number of areas.

Social networking has expanded the ways in which the public gets news and information. About a quarter (27%) of adults say they regularly or sometimes get news or news headlines through Facebook, Twitter or other social networking sites. This rises to 38% of people younger than 30, but now spans a notable share of older Americans (12% of those 65 and older) as well.

Most of those who get news from social networks (72%) say they mostly just get the same news and information they would get elsewhere. Just 27% say the news they get over social networking sites is different than the news they get elsewhere. And when asked to describe what they like about getting news over social networks and Twitter, answers range from features of the technology such as speed, portability and brevity to ways in which the content is more customized, personal and topical.

Broad Criticism of Press Performance

While the public has long been critical of many aspects of the press's performance, negative attitudes are at record levels in a number of areas. The percentage saying news organizations are often influenced by powerful people and organizations has reached an all-time high of 80%.

Other measures, including the press's perceived lack of fairness (77%), its unwillingness to admit mistakes (72%), inaccurate reporting (66%) and political bias (63%) match highs reached in 2009.

The public is about evenly divided over whether news organizations are immoral (42%) or moral (38%), but the proportion saying the press is immoral also equals an all-time high.

The percentage saying news organizations are not professional has risen 10 points since 2007.

On the positive side, majorities continue to say that news organizations care about how good a job they do (62%) and are highly professional (57%). However, the percentage saying news organizations do not care about how good a job they do (31%) is at an all-time high, while the percentage saying they are not professional (32%) equals its previous high, reached in 1999.

Long-Term Views of the Press

In the Pew Research Center's first survey on news attitudes in 1985, majorities said that news organizations were often influenced by powerful people and organizations (53%) and tended to favor one side (53%). However, by a 55% to 34% margin, more Americans said that news organizations get the facts straight than said their stories were often inaccurate.

Opinions of news organizations in all three areas have grown more negative since then. And since 2007, there have been increases in the percentages saying that news stories are often inaccurate (from 53% to 66%), that news organizations are often influenced by the powerful (from 69% to 80%), and that news organizations tend to favor one side (from 66% to 77%).

A majority (57%) views news organizations as highly professional, while 32% say they are not professional. However, the percentage saying news organizations are not professional has risen 10 points since 2007.

About six-in-ten (62%) say news organizations care about how good a job they do. However, just 18% think the media is willing to admit their mistakes; this is little changed from 2009 (21%).

By two-to-one (62% to 31%), more Americans say that news organizations are politically biased than say they are careful to avoid biased reporting. These views have changed only modestly in recent years. During the mid-1980s, far fewer said news organizations were politically biased; in Pew Research's first news attitudes survey, 45% said news organizations were politically biased while 36% said they were careful that their reporting was not politically biased.

Views of media accuracy and independence have become much more uniform across partisan groups, as Democrats and independents express increasingly critical views.

Views About the Impact of News Media

The news media also is faulted for invading people's privacy and focusing too much attention on bad news, but these opinions have not become more negative over the past quarter century. In the current survey, 69% say news organizations invade people's privacy, while 24% say they respect people's privacy. In 1985, about as many (73%) said the press invaded people's privacy.

About two-thirds of Americans (66%) say news organizations pay too much attention to bad news, while 24% say news organizations report the kinds of stories they should be covering and just 3% say the media pay too much attention to good news. These opinions have varied little over the past decade.

For the first time in a Pew Research Center survey, as many say that news organizations hurt democracy (42%) as protect democracy (42%). In the mid-1980s, about twice as many said that news organizations protect democracy rather than hurt democracy.

The public also is divided over whether news organizations stand up for America (41%) or are too critical of America (39%). These opinions have changed little in recent years, but in 2002 and 2003 somewhat more said that news organizations stand up for America.

Yet majorities have consistently expressed the view that criticism of political leaders by news organizations keeps them from doing things that should not be done. Today, 58% say this, while just 25% say that the news media's criticism keeps political leaders from doing their jobs. Even as attitudes toward the press have grown more negative, support for the press's watchdog role has remained stable.

Partisan Perceptions of the News Media

Over the past decade, Republicans have been more critical of the press's performance than have independents or Democrats. But partisan differences in a number of areas have narrowed in recent years.

Views of media accuracy and independence have become much more uniform across partisan groups, as Democrats and independents express increasingly critical views. Since 2007, the percentage of Democrats saying news organizations are often influenced by powerful people and organizations has grown by 12 points; there has been a comparable increase among independents (14 points). Meanwhile, Republicans' views have shown less change.

Even on issues where there continue to be substantial partisan differences, such as in views of political bias and whether the media is too critical of America, the gaps have narrowed.

Three-quarters of Republicans (76%) say news organizations are politically biased, a view shared by 54% of Democrats. In 2007, 70% of Republicans but only 39% of Democrats said the press was politically biased. Views on this question among independents have changed little (63% now, 61% in 2007).

Despite their declining assessments of news media, Americans say they trust the information they get from news organizations more than they trust information they get from other places, including government and business sources.

Four years ago [2007], Republicans were much more likely than Democrats to view the news media as too critical of America (63% vs. 23%). But in the current survey, far fewer Republicans (49%) say this, while the proportion of Democrats that see the press as too critical of America has grown eight points to 31%.

Democrats (64%) and independents (66%) now are about as likely as Republicans (69%) to say news media produce inaccurate stories, a notable shift from just a few years ago, when Democrats and independents had more faith in media accuracy. Partisan gaps on these two issues had been as high as 21 points for inaccuracy and 17 points for influence, but the divides have narrowed to 5 points and 4 points, respectively.

Media Trusted More than Other Sources

Despite their declining assessments of news media, Americans say they trust the information they get from news organizations more than they trust information they get from other places, including government and business sources.

The public is most inclined to believe information from local news organizations: 69% say they trust such information a lot (17%) or some (52%). Almost six-in-ten (59%) say the same about national news organizations: 14% say they trust a lot of what they learn from the national media, while 45% say they have some trust in information provided by national news organizations.

By comparison, Americans are about evenly divided over whether they trust information from the Obama administration: 50% say they trust it a lot or some, while 48% have not much or no trust in administration information. The public also is about evenly split over whether they trust information from their state governments (51% a lot or some, 47% not much or not at all). Fewer trust information from federal government agencies, business corporations or Congress. Just about three-in-ten trust a lot (1%) or some (28%) of what they learn from candidates running for office.

There are no partisan differences in how much people trust national or local news organizations. About six-in-ten Republicans (62%), Democrats (60%) and independents (58%) say they trust a lot or some of the information they get from national news organizations. Figures are higher for local media: 75% of Republicans, 68% of Democrats and 69% of independents trust at least some of the information they get from local news outlets.

Despite their negative views about the press and the accuracy and fairness of its reports, most people say they are able to find news that is accurate.

However, among Republicans and Republican-leaning independents, those who agree with the Tea Party movement express more skepticism about national media trustworthiness than do those who disagree or have no opinion of the Tea Party. Almost half of Tea Party supporters (47%) say they do not trust information from national news organizations much or at all, compared with only 31% of those who do not agree with the Tea Party or offer no opinion of it. There is no difference by Tea Party support when it comes to trust in local news organizations.

Older Americans are notably less likely to trust information from national news media: 47% say they trust information from national news organizations a lot or some; about six-in-ten in all other age groups say the same.

The Choice of News Sources

Despite their negative views about the press and the accuracy and fairness of its reports, most people say they are able to find news that is accurate. About six-in-ten (62%) say the news sources they use most generally get the facts straight; by comparison, just 25% say that news organizations generally get the facts straight.

While the vast majority of people say the press, as a whole, tends to favor one side (77%), the public is divided over whether the sources they rely on most deal fairly with all sides or not. About half (49%) say the news sources they use most tend to favor one side, but about as many (45%) say their choice sources treat all sides fairly.

There are only modest partisan differences in people's views of the accuracy and independence of the news sources they use most. . . .

News with No Point of View

More than six-in-ten Americans (63%) say they prefer news sources with no particular point of view, while 29% prefer sources that have a political point of view. The preference for news without a political point of view is even stronger when it comes to online news: 74% of those who get news online want it to come without a political point of view, while just 19% prefer online sources that have a point of view.

About as many Democrats (35%) as Republicans (31%) say they want news with a political point of view; 24% of independents say this. The partisan differences are more pronounced for online news: 32% of Democrats prefer online news with a political point of view, but just 16% of Republicans and 14% of independents want the same.

Even when the public has been asked whether they want news from *their* point of view, the clear preference is that the news have no particular point of view. In Pew Research's 2010 media consumption survey, 62% said they wanted news with no particular point of view while just 25% wanted news from their point of view.

There Is a Growing Need for Adherence to Journalistic Ethics

Clint Brewer

Clint Brewer is former president of the Society of Professional Journalists.

Journalism and the media in these days of rapidly developing digital technology, self-publishing and the incredible advances of the Internet seem like the Wild, Wild West.

Weathering the Changes

Certainly, the world has gotten smaller and access to the kind of publishing apparatus once the purview of newspaper companies that owned printing presses and broadcast companies with FCC [Federal Communications Commission] licenses has grown.

Now, individuals with access to the Web and the ability to write, report, analyze and pontificate can gain a worldwide audience if what they have to say resonates.

It is a major advance in the arena of free speech. As Wall Street and countless news reports have noted, it is putting a hurt on the returns of traditional media companies.

During these times of change, journalists will do what they can to survive. New businesses will be started, old ones may close, and staffs will be trimmed to reflect the leaner and perhaps meaner times.

I would argue to my fellow journalists, whether you are the lowliest reporter or the most powerful corporate captain, that the practice of ethical journalism is what can help separate media entities from the proverbial pack.

After a very painful process, leaders of the Society of Professional Journalists [SPJ] came out of the 1996 convention with the Society's Code of Ethics.

A Code of Ethics

Like many documents in American history that help shape the course of human events, the SPJ Code of Ethics is a simple, well-written guide. It states plainly the modern journalists' rules of engagement, and its words of wisdom are timeless—more relevant now than ever before.

Advances in technology are always supposed to make our lives easier, but that never seems to entirely be the case.

Certainly, the Internet has made publishing easier for those who wish to embark on a solo journey into the world of media. The Web has also made it easier for "staff" journalists to compete across platforms: Broadcasters can write prose, and print journalists can go in front of the camera.

The Web has also made the speed with which journalists can publish lightning quick. There is no waiting for the next newscast or tomorrow's edition. Report, write, edit, drag and drop copy and pictures. Then hit "create" or "publish" and the story "populates" your company's Web site. There is no waiting.

There is a market pendulum swinging back in the favor of ethics in journalism.

Keeping the profession's gold standard for ethics in mind can serve as a helpful counterbalance to the newfound speed with which we can publish.

The SPJ Code of Ethics asks difficult questions and makes deep demands of us on our path to publish: "seek truth and report it," "minimize harm," "act independently" "be accountable." These snippets of advice may seem like simple concepts, inherent to the journalistic process, but they are not.

As new technology puts a greater and growing ability for journalists, both staff and independent, to publish in faster and more diverse ways, we need to reconsider these tenets again and again within the context of this new world order.

The Market Value of Ethics

At the same time, our companies need to consider the value of ethical journalism not just from a moral standpoint, but also as a way to position a venture in the marketplace.

Amid the morass of celebrity news, gotcha stories, gossip and innuendo that dominate the mores and priorities of the larger media that encompasses both journalism and entertainment, I would argue there is a market pendulum swinging back in the favor of ethics in journalism.

Despite the American public's seemingly endless thirst for the tripe offered today online and more traditionally at the grocery store tabloid rack, there is also a well-documented dissatisfaction with the news media.

Study after study of the American public's feelings on their country's media for the past decade suggests severe distrust. This sentiment exists despite the tendency by media companies that own and run journalistic organs to continually pander to that lowest common denominator.

The more we give our audience what they seemingly want, the more they distrust our efforts.

I would argue that in this brave new world, there is a growing place for journalists and journalism companies to publicly hang their hats on operating under the tenets of ethical journalism. We offer our Society's Code of Ethics as that guide.

At some point, even the Wild West was conquered. At some point, our audience will en masse begin to discern the difference online between media entities that offer meaningful news and redeeming social commentary as opposed to those that simply stir the pot and appeal to our lesser angels.

Success can be found in the former as well as the latter.

Journalists Are More Ethical than People Think

Robyn Tomlin

Robyn Tomlin is the executive editor for StarNews *in Wilmington, North Carolina.*

A couple of weeks ago [November 2009], I attended a forum on the future of journalism values and ethics held at the University of Missouri's School of Journalism, the world's first journalism school. It was founded by Walter Williams, a journalist-turned-academic who wrote The Journalist's Creed, the first and perhaps definitive code of journalism ethics in 1914.

The Journalist's Creed

I'm sure I've read this code before, in school or somewhere along my career path, but I don't remember it. So, when I saw those words on a giant plaque at the front of the school and stopped to read them and think about their meaning, I was struck by how relevant they are nearly 100 years later.

Williams believed that public service was at the heart of good journalism. He wrote the code because he believed the profession should have a common set of values and that readers should hold us accountable for the methods we use to achieve them.

I know many people hold journalists in disregard. Whether for good reason or simply a function of the American public's distaste for all institutions, journalists are consistently ranked alongside lawyers and IRS [Internal Revenue Service] agents when people are asked about professionals they trust. Everyone loves to blame "The Media," and too often, that blame is well-deserved.

But when I re-read this code, I was reminded of the hundreds of honorable professionals I've had the privilege to work with over the years. I thought of these smart, passionate, ethical people who could have easily pursued more lucrative career paths. They chose journalism because they felt that by doing so they could make a difference in their communities, nation or world.

So, if journalists are so focused on public service, why is there such a gap between the public perception of the work they do and their perceptions of themselves?

Research About Journalistic Values

At the conference, we heard the results of a research study conducted by the Reynolds Journalism Institute at the University of Missouri. Mike Fancher, retired editor of the *Seattle Times*, and Esther Thorson, an associate dean and research director at the University of Missouri, presented the findings.

The premise of the research was to take several primary journalistic values and evaluate how journalists and non-journalists respond when these values are in conflict.

There wasn't a terribly large gap between the way non-journalists felt journalists should ideally respond . . . and the way journalists say they actually would respond.

Journalists and non-journalists were given ethical scenarios in which two of these values conflict, and they were asked to indicate which value should be given greater weight in each scenario.

For instance, they gave the example of a newspaper telling the story of a political race where, just before Election Day, one candidate accuses the other of having an illegitimate child. Then they asked the respondents to say whether it would be more important in this situation to "minimize harm" or to "seek the truth and report it accurately."

In other scenarios, they asked respondents to say whether it was more important to steer clear of external influences on stories or to consider the impact of the stories on people.

The results of the survey showed that while there wasn't a terribly large gap between the way non-journalists felt journalists should ideally respond to these situations and the way journalists say they actually would respond, there was a large gap between what readers thought the journalists would really do and what journalists said they do in real life.

Non-journalists placed a higher value on social responsibility than journalists did, but journalists placed a higher value on independence than did their survey counterparts.

Interestingly, both groups placed a higher value on accuracy than they did on minimizing harm to individuals.

Actions and Intentions

So what does this all mean?

Any time you pit one value against another, the decision is going to be a tough one to make.

Over time, we have developed policies and institutional norms that help us to be consistent in the way we navigate these choppy waters, but even these fail us at times.

I think journalists need to do a better job of explaining themselves and telling readers why values like independence are important to preserve.

We probably also need to do a better job of listening to readers' concerns when we are making these tough decisions.

Finally, I believe we need to go back to our foundational values and ensure that our actions are consistent with the values we say we hold dear. In other words, our actions need to match our intentions. When they don't, we need to be prepared to explain ourselves.

Walter Williams' prescient statement of journalistic belief stands as an inspirational model. More than anything, it reminds us that, in this day and age, when anyone can disseminate information and opinion, some people still believe that journalism is a public service, first and foremost.

That is a value worth fighting to preserve.

News Organizations Are in Need of New Ethics Guidelines for Journalists

Kelly McBride

Kelly McBride is senior faculty specializing in media ethics at The Poynter Institute, a journalism school in St. Petersburg, Florida.

[National Public Radio (NPR) vice president] Ellen Weiss' resignation wasn't about Juan Williams [NPR political analyst] and it wasn't about NPR. It was about a news organization trying to keep a star in orbit by bending its standards. And there are plenty of other professional news outlets in similar positions, places where one journalist can take on a side job as a commentator while his colleagues worry about what they can share with their friends on Facebook.

Buried in last week's [January 6, 2011] announcement was news that the public radio company is reviewing its code of ethics. If newsroom leaders around the country honestly assessed their own operations, they'd find that most of them have outdated, unclear ethics policies, which they apply inconsistently. That is, those with policies.

The Need for Clear Policies

Why is that? First there are the *obvious* reasons. Journalists do their jobs differently today in response to advancing technology, changes in audience expectations and economic devastation.

Then there are the *really obvious* reasons. Journalism is a profession rife with stars who get away with a lot. And in this new environment, stars tend to have more opportunities than ever, while newsroom leaders don't always have the resources to pay their stars enough money to lock them down exclusively or the time to manage their potential conflicts of interest and competing loyalties.

"The climate has changed a whole bunch," Bill Marimow told me Friday in a phone conversation. Besides once being a senior news executive at NPR, he was editor of *The* (Baltimore) *Sun* and *The Philadelphia Inquirer*.

"In some cases, people who were truly outstanding become almost like franchises," said Marimow, who after years of running newsrooms, *and occasionally being removed himself*, has recently gone back to reporting at *The Inquirer*.

Opinionating has grown substantially in the world of journalism, courtesy of talk radio, blogging, and especially cable TV, which pays its opinionators big bucks.

Until he became Washington bureau chief for the *Daily Beast*, Howard Kurtz covered media for *The Washington Post* while simultaneously hosting CNN's Sunday morning roundup show, "Reliable Sources." He covered CNN for the *Post* while he was being paid by CNN.

The *New York Times'* Nicholas Kristof has morphed from a columnist into his own social advocacy movement with his Half the Sky agenda.

And *Detroit Free Press* sports writer Mitch Albom pioneered the multi-gig life, working for ESPN, a local radio station and freelancing for *Sports Illustrated*.

As if this isn't complicated enough, opinionating has grown substantially in the world of journalism, courtesy of talk radio, blogging, and especially cable TV, which pays its opinionators big bucks. And they don't want some guy nobody's heard of spouting opinions. They want a star.

Even when there aren't direct conflicts of interests, there are competing styles and loyalties. . . .

"Juan [Williams] was in this weird space where he was going to cable news in prime time, where opinion is all they do, then coming back to NPR which is a more traditional news service," Eric Deggans said by phone Friday morning. He's the TV and media critic at the *St. Petersburg Times*, which Poynter [Institute] owns.

There have to be clear delineations between those who can and can't opine. Then a policy must articulate what range of opinions will be tolerated.

Defining Roles to Minimize Conflict

Newsroom leaders must first delineate between reporters and columnists, Marimow said. Some expert reporters find themselves with the title of analyst or commentator when opportunity knocks. That was originally how NPR attempted to manage Williams, by changing his job from correspondent (which is more like a reporter) to analyst (which is more like a columnist).

"Every newsroom should be thinking about this stuff," Deggans said. "Every newsroom has stars that they make exceptions for. That's why this stuff doesn't get codified."

Or it gets codified, then ignored. I often get calls from newsroom leaders struggling to retrofit an old ethics policy to new activities. In an environment where roles and responsibilities seem to change every couple of months, some newsrooms have given up trying to write down guidelines or provide the training necessary to apply written guidelines.

That leaves the staff, both the stars and the rest of the journalists, wondering where the boundaries are and what the process is for discovering them.

NPR has a good lineup of outside advisors and internal people to help them do this, including Poynter's Bob Steele. I've no doubt that they will have significant discussions about how journalists uphold traditional standards while they thrive and stay relevant in the modern world.

It will be tough to write guidelines that allow the rock stars of journalism to pursue opportunity and extend their influence, while preserving their primary loyalty to one central newsroom. "They have to get the language just right," Marimow said.

That means there have to be clear delineations between those who can and can't opine. Then a policy must articulate what range of opinions will be tolerated. "I think a good policy will encourage a broad latitude of opinions," he said.

The Goal for a Code of Ethics

Raul Ramirez, news director at San Francisco public radio station KQED, is part of the committee reviewing NPR's code of ethics. Although he didn't want to discuss that process, he wrote the code for his own station and has helped other newsrooms review their codes. His goal in creating such policies is to create a document that can continually incorporate new challenges.

David Cohn, founder of the crowdfunded journalism site Spot.Us, is also part of the committee. "Ethics is not a math equation where you always get the same answer," he said. "We're going to come up with guidelines and principles. It will be up to NPR to figure out how to interpret those."

When it comes to other NPR talent, it's too early in the process to determine what language the committee will recommend. The Chairman of NPR's board, David Edwards, told my colleague Mallary Tenore that he didn't know what limits would be placed on other talent.

"I think it would be wrong for me or anyone to say or to know what the outcome will be," he said. "These are core discussions that I suspect NPR and other news organizations really have to grapple with, and that's what this committee has to do."

Ramirez and Cohn both said they hope to help NPR create a useful tool. Ramirez said he uses KQED's written code of ethics as talking points in the day-to-day running of the newsroom, so that core values stay top of mind.

"There are so many more opportunities for reporters and editors to collaborate, creating a stronger product," he said. "Our reputation, and the trust of our audience, is only as strong as the weakest link in our newsroom."

That should be strong motivation for managers to do what it takes to build strong relationships, Marimow said. He's managed a number of stars, including columnist Steve Lopez and investigative reporter Mark Bowden.

"I don't think I've ever had stars that I found unmanageable," he said. "Because we all started as reporters, there was a mutual respect."

After a well-written policy and good training, that goes a long way.

There Is a Need for More Discussion About Ethics in Advertising

Rance Crain

Rance Crain is president of Crain Communications and editor-in-chief of Advertising Age, Crain's Chicago Business, Crain's New York Business, *and* TelevisionWeek.

Maybe you have to live in a society with longstanding repressive traditions to give much thought to the social and ethical implications of advertising.

When I visited Russia several years ago, I learned consumers there are influenced by two great traditions: the czars of the 18th century and communism. Both the czars and the communists operated under the assumption that "your confusion is my victory," and so yes is no and black is white. "The evil is not a bad product, but advertising that gives the opportunity to choose bad things," a Russian educator said.

Because advertising in Russia is a relatively new force, and most consumers regard it with the same disbelief as communism, there is much more discussion about its place in society.

I came back from Russia thinking about how we should emulate the Russians in this regard. I said at the time: "There's too much advertising that borders on misleading and even unethical, and as my old boss Stan Cohen says, these excesses could lead to the coming of a new Ralph Nader." I wrote this back in 2007 before our near financial collapse.

Yet none of the ethical considerations of blatantly excessive sales pitches were discussed during or after the housing meltdown. The sad truth is that many financial marketers didn't want prospective home buyers and mortgage holders to understand the downside of the transactions—that interest rates can go up without notice, that buyers were taking on too much debt, that housing prices don't always go up.

What obligation did advertisers have in pointing out the realities of the marketplace? And what obligations did individual practitioners have to themselves to bring any doubts they may have had to their superiors? And then, if their doubts rang on deaf ears, to walk away from their job of disseminating misleading information?

A Time for Ethical Debate

That's why I believe it's high time for the ad industry to formalize the process of ethical debate and discussion—to bring up issues that many people in the business would rather not talk about.

It's important for ad people to feel comfortable talking about the ethics of their own behavior, but it's evident that many were not doing so when the American Advertising Federation and the University of Missouri announced the formation of the Institute for Advertising Ethics.

A heightened sense of ethics will help give courage to people questioning whether they're doing the right thing.

We received a dozen or so mostly skeptical comments when we broke the news. "A total waste of money and a feel-good 'look at what we're doing to police ourselves' exercise in futility," said one commentator. "All we need to know about ethics we probably learned from our mother," he added (the writer signed his name Rob).

What concerns me is that we seem resigned to making the same mistakes over and over again. Does anybody really think that increased regulatory scrutiny will prevent the next financial debacle or oil spill? What we need is a frank discussion of the ethical issues involved, even if some people think such conversations are naïve (as one of our readers said).

The Benefits of Ethics

Wally Snyder, executive director of the institute, pointed out that there are sound business reasons for putting advertising ethics front and center. In research conducted by students of Missouri's Reynolds Journalism School, consumers said they'd be more likely to buy products if the company marketing it were ethical. "Honest advertising" was the top-ranked attribute that would make a company ethical, consumers surveyed indicated.

But maybe more important in the long run, a heightened sense of ethics will help give courage to people questioning whether they're doing the right thing. The student research directed at ad practitioners disclosed that they'd be more inclined to voice their concerns if they were given "permission" to speak up by their superiors.

Listen, we're in a first-class mess in this country, with people thinking that nothing works and nothing can be done about it. One small step is to start a discussion about doing the right thing, and I'm very glad that the advertising industry is leading the way.

CHAPTER 2

Should Telling the Truth Take Precedence over Other Ethical Concerns?

Chapter Preface

According to the *Society of Professional Journalists (SPJ) Code of Ethics*, the duty of the journalist is to inform the public by "seeking truth and providing a fair and comprehensive account of events and issues." Truthfulness is a value within this code, as are fairness and comprehensiveness. Elsewhere in the code, journalists are urged to "show good taste" and "avoid conflicts of interest." When these values come into conflict, it is up to a journalist to determine what to do. Journalists are regularly faced with situations in which upholding the value of truthfulness cannot be accomplished without compromising on one or more other values. Regarding these varied situations, people differ widely on the right action to take.

Among various ethical conflicts are two key areas in which truthfulness can create an ethical dilemma for journalists. The first is in determining what should become news in the first place; a story's being real does not necessarily mean it warrants news coverage. However, the public's taste for lurid stories, combined with the need to sell newspapers, subscriptions, or advertising, pushes journalists to report any true story that will attract readers. But what if that story is about a private citizen going through a private difficulty? Does public interest alone justify reporting it?

The *SPJ Code* states, "Only an overriding public need can justify intrusion into anyone's privacy." In 2009 a fifth-grade teacher in California accidentally inserted private sexual video footage into a class DVD distributed to students. Several news outlets reported the story, and some showed video footage with obscene parts censored, and some named the teacher. It could be argued that the public has a right to know about the incident and the video because a public school teacher is involved. But it could also be argued that the event was an embarrassing accident for the teacher that does not justify media exposure. With this incident a journalist is asked to balance truth with other values—such as privacy—in determining whether to report the story at all, whether to name the teacher, and whether to show any part of the video.

The second key area in which truthfulness can create an ethical dilemma for journalists concerns how news material is acquired. If the ultimate goal is to inform the public with factual reports, does it matter how these news stories are acquired? This issue comes up in the case of undercover reporting, in which journalists purposely misrepresent themselves for the purpose of gaining access to people or information. The *SPJ Code* states: "Avoid undercover or other surreptitious methods of gathering information except when traditional open methods will not yield information vital to the public." Yet, as is clear in this chapter, journalists disagree about whether undercover journalism is ethical. Even without going undercover, however, journalists have many opportunities in which a lack of truthfulness may help them gain information.

Journalists may make promises they cannot keep in order to gain information. In many cases, people who are promised anonymity are inclined to disclose certain privileged information to journalists. Promising anonymity puts the journalist in the position of protecting the identity of the informant in the future, even when the journalist is pressed to disclose this information. Is making a promise one knows one may be unable to keep justified by the greater good of gaining information for a news story? The *SPJ Code* urges journalists to "keep promises." However, it also notes that journalists have "a special obligation to ensure that the public's business is conducted in the open and that government records are open to inspection." Does this special obligation justify a promise of anonymity to a government insider, even if one is unsure of one's ability to keep that promise? Here, once again, the value of truthfulness comes in conflict with other values.

To say that journalists have a professional and ethical obligation to tell the truth is fairly uncontroversial. When truthfulness conflicts with other values, however, it is not always clear whether truth should prevail. The authors of the viewpoints in this chapter explore some of the dilemmas faced by journalists in the pursuit of truth.

The First Amendment Enables Journalists to Publish Unpopular Truths

Tim Wu

Tim Wu is a professor at Columbia Law School and serves as senior advisor to the Federal Trade Commission.

It is time for the United States to drop the case against WikiLeaks. Pressing forward with efforts to prosecute an Internet publisher at home while standing up for an open Internet in Egypt and the world at large is an increasingly tenuous position. The WikiLeaks case endangers the reputation of the United States as a defender of free speech and an open Internet globally, while forcing the [Barack] Obama administration to take uncomfortable constitutional positions better suited to the [Richard] Nixon administration. The importance of this issue is hard to overstate: At a time when the Internet is increasingly recognized as a medium of global resistance to authoritarian rule and when protestors in Tahrir square [Egypt] are holding up signs that say "Thank you, Facebook!", the Obama administration and the United States must make sure that they stand on the right side.

The Allegation of Conspiracy

The timing is important. Just over a year ago [January 2010], Secretary of State Hillary Clinton paved the way with her notable speech on "Internet Freedom." More recently, she explicitly condemned Egypt's Internet shutdown. Her message—that an open Internet is an issue of fundamental freedom in the 21st century—has been complicated by the actions of other branches of the U.S. federal government, especially the Justice Department's plans to prosecute WikiLeaks for its role in publishing leaked U.S. State Department diplomatic cables.

While the Justice Department's original plan to rely on the Espionage Act apparently has been dropped, it is still considering the prosecution of either Julian Assange [founder and editor-in-chief of WikiLeaks] personally or media organizations that published documents obtained by Wikileaks based on a theory of conspiracy or solicitation.

If the First Amendment stands for anything, it is that a government's dislike for individuals' speech ought not be taken as legal grounds for their imprisonment.

Yet so far, no clear evidence has emerged that would support an allegation that anyone in the media conspired with Bradley Manning, the alleged leaker who is already in military prison, to obtain documents. Unfortunately, that won't necessarily stop the Justice Department since as every prosecutor knows, conspiracy is relatively easy to allege, requiring nothing more than some evidence of an agreement to commit a crime and an overt act by one of the conspirators (Manning, in this case). When you think about it, publication nearly always requires some kind of agreement. The federal statutes' broad definition of conspiracy is what makes it so dangerous.

The First Amendment

Needless to say, labeling the act of publishing a criminal conspiracy would be a strong challenge to the U.S. Constitution's First Amendment's protections.

I should state that I have no particular sympathy for Assange or his website's activities. But if the First Amendment stands for anything, it is that a government's dislike for individuals' speech ought not be taken as legal grounds for their imprisonment.

WikiLeaks and Assange are unpopular and even hated in some circles. Senator Joe Lieberman, were he president, would long ago have begun the extradition. "I think it's the most serious violation of the Espionage Act in our history," he recently told FOX News. But let's not let the impulse to punish WikiLeaks indict not just Mr. Assange but the editors of the *New York Times*, sympathetic bloggers, and anyone else around the world who mirrors leaked materials.

Prosecution of WikiLeaks would hurt, if it not destroy, the credibility of the United States in claiming to be the world's most vital advocate of an open Internet. It would send the dangerous signal that the United States only claims to uphold the virtues of an open Internet and free speech—until it decides it doesn't like a particular website. There could hardly be a worse moment to send that message, to be telling the Arab world: Do as we say, not as we do.

Upholding the U.S. Constitution

Foreign concerns aside, the Obama administration must also consider its own duties to uphold the Constitution. Lest we forget, the last administration to champion the view that the publishers of leaked materials are criminals was, of course, the Nixon administration, which took this position in the 1971 Pentagon Papers case—and lost. Were it to go forward, the prosecution of WikiLeaks would force the Obama administration to go to court and argue that First Amendment protects only certain kinds of speech. While Nixon himself would certainly be pleased to hear that Barack Obama has adopted his campaign against the First Amendment, I sincerely doubt Obama's supporters feel that way.

For the Obama administration, there lies a real danger here of repeating the mistakes made by the previous White House. George W. Bush's team believed that the United States could disregard human rights when it was convenient and somehow still maintain America's international reputation as the foremost agent of freedom and democracy. The Bushies were wrong. Let's hope Obama's team won't make the same mistake. As the saying goes, if you want to talk the talk, it helps to walk the walk.

Undercover Reporting Is a Legitimate Method to Gain Information

Aaron Swartz

Aaron Swartz is the founder and director of Demand Progress, a nonprofit political action group, and founder of the website Watchdog.net.

This past February [2007], the famed lobbying firm APCO was approached by a man named Kenneth Case. Case said he represented the Maldon Group, an obscure firm that wished to improve the public image of Turkmenistan, where it had some investments. It was nothing out of the ordinary—private firms often lobby on behalf of foreign countries, either because they think it will increase the value of their investments or because they are acting as a front for the foreign government.

An Undercover Piece on Lobbying

APCO happily met with them, despite the fact that the Stalinist regime of Turkmenistan is one of the most noxious on the planet, after North Korea. In a recent report, Human Rights Watch called it "one of the most repressive and authoritarian [governments] in the world," noting it had "untold numbers of political prisoners . . . draconian restrictions on freedom of expression . . . [and] foreign travel restrictions."

All of which would normally be considered just another day of doing business in D.C., except for one thing: "Kenneth Case" was a fiction, and his "Maldon Group" a ruse cooked up by *Harper's* magazine editor Ken Silverstein to demonstrate what D.C. lobbying was really like.

The resulting piece, "Their Men in Washington," won immediate acclaim. Silverstein was interviewed on everything from NPR [National Public Radio] to Al-Jazeera, and the article quickly became widely linked and reposted in the blogosphere. It gave a rare look at the inner workings of public relations firms, from how they pitched themselves to prospective clients to the little-known behind the scenes work they offered to do.

> *More surprising was the response from the supposed arbiters of journalistic ethics.*

APCO proposed laundering money through academic groups to fund congressional delegations or special conferences, as well as hiring "think-tank experts who would say, 'On the one hand this and the other hand that,'" writing pieces for them to sign and placing them as op-eds [opinion pieces] in major newspapers. Meanwhile, Cassidy & Associates, another lobbying firm hoping to receive the Turkmenistan account, bragged that they had "strong personal relationships" at every major level of government and had recently succeeded in keeping Equatorial Guinea's dictator Teodoro Obiang off the list of the world's Top 10 dictators.

Opposition to Undercover Reporting

Not everyone, however, was happy to have this information made public. APCO sent their PR people into damage control, issuing a press release insisting "Silverstein's charade is a comment on his ethics, not ours. [His] claim that he was working in the 'public interest' [because going undercover was] the only way he could get information is as false as his story." APCO also insisted that Silverstein's "suggestion" that APCO offered to get others to work secretly on behalf of Turkmenistan could not be true because "current law REQUIRES disclosure" in such situations (emphasis in original).

In an NPR discussion between Ken Silverstein and APCO representative B. Jay Cooper, Cooper justified taking Turkmenistan as a client because, before doing so, they'd run the idea past their contacts in the government and they thought it would be a positive development. He also explained that writing op-eds and getting other people to sign on to them was standard practice—he'd done it dozens of times, for example. Cassidy & Associates, the more expensive firm, did little to respond to Silverstein's charges in the press. Seeing APCO's "defense," this seems like a wise choice.

Of course, it's not surprising that the companies exposed would be opposed to the article. More surprising was the response from the supposed arbiters of journalistic ethics. CBS's Public Eye blog insisted that the operation was inappropriate because everyone already knows that lobbyists deceive the public about their clients. "When you indulge in subterfuge to merely provide the conventional wisdom with a concrete example," they wrote, "that's when the cost ... isn't worth the benefit."

Bill Buzenberg, the executive director of the Center for Public Integrity, an independent investigative reporting group, told reporters that "misrepresenting yourself is not a good idea. We're with Howard Kurtz on this one." Kurtz, media critic for the *Washington Post* and CNN, had sided with APCO in a *Post* column titled "Stung by *Harper's* in a Web of Deceit."

Kurtz reported that the editor of *Harper's* defended the practice by pointing to "a long history of sting operations" by journalists. But, Kurtz wrote, "that undercover tradition has faded in recent years. No newspaper today would do what the *Chicago Sun-Times* did in the 1970s. . . . Fewer television programs are doing what ABC did in the 1990s. . . . NBC's *Date-*

line joins in stings against child predators, but by tagging along with law enforcement officials."

Why this decline in undercover reporting? Kurtz had an explanation: "The reason is that, no matter how good the story, lying to get it raises as many questions about journalists as their subjects." But maybe that isn't the whole story.

A History of Undercover Reporting

Undercover reporting has a storied history. Nellie Bly, famous for traveling around the world in 80 days, also did a famed investigation of the conditions in insane asylums for the *New York World*. Bly feigned insanity for a series of physicians before being committed to a lunatic asylum. There she documented rotten and spoiled food, freezing living conditions, frigid bathwater, abusive nurses and relatively sane fellow residents. "What, excepting torture, would produce insanity quicker than this treatment?" she wondered. The series, later published as the book *Ten Days in a Mad-House*, created a sensation, and Bly was asked to join a government investigation of asylum conditions.

More recently, as Kurtz points out, Chicago in the 1970s and 1980s was something of a golden era of undercover reporting, in no small part because of the efforts of one woman: Pam Zekman. She and her investigative crew at WBBM-TV used undercover reporting to break dozens of stories. She got a job at a nursing home so she could verify allegations of filth and mistreatment made by relatives.

She got a job as a dance instructor to prove a local dance studio was cheating money from seniors. She had a team work at an abortion clinic to prove they were performing abortions on women who weren't pregnant. And she had a staffer apply for a job at the airport to see what kind of background checks they did on bag screeners.

But Zekman's biggest story came while she worked at the *Chicago Sun-Times*. Everyone knew Chicago's government was corrupt, but Zekman proved it. She purchased a seedy tavern on Chicago's Near North Side with "more code violations than barstools," renamed it the Mirage Tavern, and recorded everything as a long string of officials—the fire inspector, the plumbing inspector, the ventilation inspector, the county clerk, accountants, landlords—took bribes while overlooking violations. Even the people who maintained the pinball machine dropped by to show the management how to skim profits.

Undercover reporting has largely dried up in recent years.

The resulting 25-part series was full of juicy details like the "business broker" who advised them to bribe everyone except cops, because cops "keep coming around every month, like flies, looking for a payoff." It led to a stream of tourists visiting the bar, and hundreds calling the paper with new tips. There was coverage in outlets like *Time* and *60 Minutes*, and in newspapers from Denmark to Australia. A federal investigation of the inspectors quickly led to indictments for 29 electrical inspectors, while the Illinois Revenue Department created a 12-man "Mirage Audit Unit."

In more recent years, Barbara Ehrenreich went undercover for *Harper's* as a maid, a waiter, a Wal-Mart employee and a nursing home assistant. She argued that such "unskilled" jobs were much harder than the white-collar work she was used to and found that even working by herself, eating little, and living in pitiful conditions, she still was unable to make ends meet. The result was the bestselling book *Nickel and Dimed*, which led to a resurgence of interest in the conditions of the "working poor."

The Impact of Lawsuits

But, outside of *Harper's*, undercover reporting has largely dried up in recent years, and many point to the Food Lion case as the reason. In 1992, *ABC's PrimeTime Live* sent reporters undercover at the Food Lion grocery store to investigate claims of unsanitary food handling practices. The reporters falsified their resumes ("I really miss working in a grocery store. . . . I would love to make a career with the company," one wrote on her application), donned hidden camera rigs and got the story.

The pictures were vivid [according to the *Columbia Journalism Review*]: "old meat being redated and put out again for sale, old ground beef being mixed with new, out-of-date chicken getting a coating of barbecue sauce before being relaunched in the gourmet section." Viewers came away convinced of Food Lion's wrongdoing.

But Food Lion fought back, filing a lawsuit against ABC—not challenging the accuracy of the story (although they did do that in public), but charging the reporters who got it with dishonesty. The chain sued ABC for fraud (for lying on their application), trespassing (for coming to Food Lion without permission) and breach of loyalty (for videotaping bad practices when they were supposed to be working for the company). After years of legal wrangling, in 1997 a jury awarded Food Lion a $5.5 million verdict. In 1999, the case was overturned on appeal on somewhat technical grounds.

But by then it was too late—the case had been grinding through the legal system for nearly seven years, and journalists and news outlets had gotten the message: undercover reporting has serious costs. Looking back in 1997, the editor of the *Columbia Journalism Review* declared the 1990s "a humbling time for journalism, particularly investigative television journalism." Among those humbled: *20/20* had to pay $10 million for claiming BankAtlantic Financial had hoodwinked investors, the Minnesota News Council upheld a complaint against a Minneapolis TV station for painting "a distorted, untruthful picture" of Northwest Airlines safety practices, a Houston TV station paid $5.5 million for charging a state representative with an insurance scam, Michael Moore's *TV Nation* paid $5 million for claiming a company had spread toxic sludge over a Texas ranch.

"You can expect journalists in the wake of this to give us more stories about Dennis Rodman and Madonna instead of more stories that are important to us," 1st Amendment lawyer Bruce Sanford said at the time of the Food Lion case. "The specter of a verdict of this magnitude . . . will have a chilling effect on investigative journalists all over the country," proclaimed Jane Kirtley, then executive director of the Reporters Committee on Freedom of the Press.

Investigative journalism has gotten so rare that foundations have stepped into the gap.

A Decline in Investigative Journalism

They appear to have been right (although, thankfully, the spate of Dennis Rodman stories has since abated). Undercover reporting has fallen out of fashion. Ken Silverstein argues that this is because reporters, especially Washington reporters, have grown complacent. In an *L.A. Times* op-ed on the controversy, he wrote:

> The decline of undercover reporting—and of investigative reporting in general reflects, in part, the increasing conservatism and cautiousness of the media, especially the smug, high-end Washington press corps. As reporters have grown more socially prominent during the last several decades, they've become part of the very power structure that they're supposed to be tracking and scrutinizing.

The piece on lobbyists, he and his editor insist, was not just done to investigate the particular lobbying firms, but to reawaken journalists to the power of undercover reporting. "There was this meta level in the planning that asked, 'How will the journalism establishment react?'" *Harper's* editor Roger

Hodge told a reporter. "The fact that undercover journalism has fallen out of fashion seems to be a problem with the profession."

Investigative journalism has gotten so rare that foundations have stepped into the gap. A collection of funders has joined to form the new nonprofit ProPublica, which will have an annual budget of $10 million, already making it the largest investigative journalism team in the country.

It's unclear if anything will wake news organizations from their slumber. Perhaps someone should go undercover inside them to find out.

Journalists Should Always Aim to Provide the Truth, Not Just the Facts

Linda Greenhouse

Linda Greenhouse is a senior research scholar at Yale Law School and former US Supreme Court reporter for The New York Times.

A story in the *New York Times* about a dispute involving the Fox News Channel described Fox News as "a channel with a reputation for having a conservative point of view in much of its programming."

Really?!

That phrase "with a reputation" put the reporter, and the newspaper, at arm's length from the fact that the Fox News channel does have a conservative point of view, and proudly so.

What was the purpose of that distancing phrase?

A *Washington Post* article on the shooting at the Fort Hood Army base recounted that the shooter, Nidal Hasan, "allegedly opened fire"—an act that he indisputably performed in front of dozens of witnesses.

A *New York Times* article, typical of many others, referred to Jared Loughner as "the man accused of opening fire outside a Tucson supermarket." Whether the Tucson shooter is guilty of murder is a legal question, but there is no question at all about his identity as the man who shot Congresswoman [Gabrielle] Giffords and killed six people. We don't have to say "accused of"—he did the deed in front of dozens of witnesses.

I'm not picking on the *New York Times*—the newspaper I read most carefully—as well as the place I worked for 40 years. And although it is attacked, most often from the right but not infrequently from the left, for various kinds of bias, it actually, in both its performance and its ideals, epitomizes the commitment of mainstream journalism to the goals of fairness and objectivity.

There has been a lively debate going on for years over whether the "he said, she said" format . . . impedes rather than enhances the goal of informing the reader.

This is nothing new. Adolph Ochs, the founding publisher of the modern *New York Times*, whose byword was "without fear or favor," believed that a responsible newspaper should "report all sides of a controversial issue, and let the reader decide the truth," according to a reminiscence written a couple of years ago for internal distribution to the *Times* staff. His successor, Arthur Hays Sulzberger, liked to say: "We tell the public which way the cat is jumping. The public will take care of the cat."

The "He Said, She Said" Format

In my remarks, I would like to raise some questions about the assumption behind that credo, as well as the utility, in this media-saturated and cynical age, of the siren call of "fairness and objectivity." I will do this by examining how these standards are working in practice. I will question whether the working definition of "fairness," which seems to boil down to "give both sides of every story," can operate in a complex world where many stories worth telling have many sides—or only one.

I am hardly the first one to raise questions like these. Inside the profession of journalism, there has been a lively debate going on for years over whether the "he said, she said" format, designed to avoid taking sides on contentious issues, impedes rather than enhances the goal of informing the reader.

This debate comes up most often during political campaigns, and many press critics and commentators have pointed out how superficial and subject to manipulation that format can be in the context of a campaign.

For that reason, many news organizations now publish or post "fact-check" boxes that vet the accuracy of political ads or of candidates' assertions during debates. A good example of this was a "Check Point" feature that ran in the *Times* during the last presidential campaign under the headline: "Ad on Sex Education Distorts Obama Policy."

It reported that claims in an ad being run by the [John] McCain campaign "seriously distort the record" by portraying Barack Obama as favoring "comprehensive sex education" for kindergarten students.

Another campaign story, which ran in the *Times* as straight news on page one, reported that the author of a negative book about Sen. John Kerry's war record that appeared during the 2004 presidential campaign was now trying with a newly published book to inflict equivalent damage on Senator Obama. But "several of the book's accusations, in fact, are unsubstantiated, misleading or inaccurate," the article declared, flatly.

A Binary Example

It's relatively easy to make a frontal attack on the "he said, she said" norm in the context of a political campaign, where there is widespread agreement about the format's inadequacy. It's more challenging in other contexts. For instance, some people—many people—consider waterboarding to be torture, and they refer to it that way. But others cling to the notion that it is not torture. What is a news organization to do?

National Public Radio [NPR] has chosen to use "harsh interrogation tactics" or "enhanced interrogation techniques" instead of "torture" when reporting stories about waterboarding and other coercive practices used to interrogate terrorism suspects.

When listeners pushed back, the NPR ombudsman, Alicia C. Shepard, responded that she agreed with the network. "The problem is that the word torture is loaded with political and social implications," she wrote on her blog, adding: "NPR's job is to give listeners all perspectives, and present the news as detailed as possible and put it in context." Because using the word torture would amount to taking sides, reporters should instead "describe the techniques and skip the characterization entirely," she said.

Again, that may be an easy example, because it's binary—use the word torture, or avoid it. How about a complex event or situation that requires the reporter to make a series of judgments in order to describe adequately and assign priorities to such factors as motivation, relationships among actors or likely consequences.

The Society of Professional Journalists dropped "objectivity" from its ethics code.

The Aim for Objectivity

Paul Taylor, a former political reporter for the *Washington Post*, had this to say in his trenchant book, *See How They Run*:

> "Sometimes I worry that my squeamishness about making sharp judgments, pro or con, makes me unfit for the small-bank world of daily journalism. Other times I conclude that it makes me ideally suited for newspapering—certainly for the rigors and conventions of modern 'objective' journalism. For I can dispose of my dilemmas by writing stories straight down the middle. I can search for the halfway point between the best and the worst that might be said about someone (or some policy or idea) and write my story in that fair-minded place. By aiming for the golden mean, I probably land near the best approximation of truth more often than if I were guided by any other set of compasses—partisan,

ideological, psychological, whatever . . . Yes, I am seeking truth. But I'm also seeking refuge. I'm taking a pass on the toughest calls I face."

Jay Rosen, a press critic and journalism professor at New York University, calls the phenomenon that Paul Taylor describes as "regression toward a phony mean."

[Journalist] Joan Didion, way back in 1996, referred to "fairness" as a "familiar newsroom piety" and "benign ideal" that operates in practice as "the excuse for a good deal of autopilot reporting and lazy thinking." What it often means, she wrote, "is a scrupulous passivity, an agreement to cover the story not as it is occurring but as it is presented, which is to say as it is manufactured."

How about truth for a goal?

In that same year, 1996, the Society of Professional Journalists dropped "objectivity" from its ethics code, a development understood to reflect the fact that there had ceased to be, if there ever was, a common understanding within the profession of what objective reporting consists of.

The Alternative to Fairness and Balance

A leading commentary on the modern practice of journalism, *The Elements of Journalism*, by Bill Kovach and Tom Rosenstiel, omits "fairness" and "objectivity" from its list of the 10 basic elements of journalism, described as "clear principles that journalists agree on—and that citizens have a right to expect."

Why the omissions? "Familiar and even useful" as the idea of fairness and balance may be, the authors say, the very concept "has been so mangled" as to have become part of journalism's problem, rather than a solution to perceived problems of bias and partiality. But Brent Cunningham, managing editor of the *Columbia Journalism Review*, has observed that despite this discontent and self-reflection, "nothing replaced objectivity as journalism's dominant norm."

In fact, he notes, "a cottage industry of bias police has sprung up," leading to "hypersensitivity among the press to charges of bias," which in turn reinforces the problematic adherence to a standard of "objectivity" that "can trip us up on the way to 'truth.'" Truth. How about truth for a goal?

"We may not have a journalism of truth because we haven't demanded one," the cultural critic Neal Gabler wrote in response to the media's performance in covering the health care debate. He noted that by simply reporting the latest guided missile from Sarah Palm or Rush Limbaugh, the media "marshal facts, but they don't seek truth. They behave as if every argument must be heard and has equal merit, when some are simply specious."

He added that those who seek a platform know that the mainstream media will refrain from serving as a referee for fear of being accused of taking sides. The result, Gabler concluded, is a journalism of "silly reportorial ping-pong at best and badly misleading information at worst."

The Role of the Interviewer

One of broadcast television's most acclaimed news programs, the *NewsHour with Jim Lehrer*, unfortunately has come to exemplify this problem. It almost never presents a point of view without, in the same segment, providing a platform for the opposite view, and its moderators often sit passively as the panelists rebut one another. Viewers have recently begun to complain about this format.

Michael Getler, the Public Broadcasting System's [PBS's] ombudsman, wrote in 2008 that the complaining viewers have a point. He said there were too many segments "in which Democratic and Republican strategists simply contradict each other, often leaving the viewing audience numb and angry.

There are simply too many of these in which the viewer is sacrificed on the altar of 'balanced' news coverage that actually does not inform."

The "key to making these segments useful is the interviewer," he said, "who must be prepared to challenge guests, not just with the other person's opinion, but with facts and alternative analysis that helps viewers judge what is being said. Challenge and confrontation often does not seem to be in the *NewsHour* playbook."

Getler's criticism has gone largely unheeded inside the *NewsHour*. During the health care debate in Congress, Judy Woodruff, the moderator of a segment on the subject, failed to challenge a series of unsupported assertions made by a guest, the former Republican Congressman and House majority leader Dick Armey, a leading critic of health-care reform.

Why is it just so difficult to make the search for truth the highest journalistic value?

(Digression—note that the mainstream media refrained from using the word "reform," instead often using the unwieldy phrase "health-care overhaul," "overhaul" being regarded in the newsroom as a neutral word while "reform" implies that what is being proposed is better than what currently exists.)

Viewers complained to Michael Getler, the PBS ombudsman, who passed the complaints on to the program's executive producer. The producer, noting that Ms. Woodruff had turned to the other guest, a reform advocate named Richard Kirsch, to invite a reply, responded in defense of the moderator: "Seems to me the guests were asked to rebut one another. Judy was the moderator, not the judge."

Getler said in his column that the incident raised the question "of whether moderators, if not serving as judges, need to at least challenge guests more forcefully, especially on subjects such as health care where the degree of falsehoods and fear-mongering has reached very high levels, so that the viewer has a better chance of getting at least close to the truth."

The Problem with Truth

There's that pesky word "truth" again. Why is it just so difficult to make the search for truth the highest journalistic value? Well, for one thing, the notion that there exists one Truth to be spoken or published exists in some tension with core First Amendment values. After all, "the First Amendment recognizes no such thing as a 'false' idea," the Supreme Court tells us. The familiar image of the marketplace of ideas suggests ideas competing freely for public favor, unvetted, unranked, and unregulated by some superintending power.

> *The he-said, she-said format is increasingly the best that a reporter can do under the severe time pressure of being required to file continuous updates for a website.*

For another thing, the word "truth" lacks a single definition. To report, without elaboration, a politician's charge concerning the "death panels" in the health-care bill is—assuming the politician is quoted accurately—certainly to report the truth. Does such a report convey a more useful or meaningful truth, the contextual truth of the situation? Obviously not. But just as obviously, it would not require a correction.

In their book, *The Elements of Journalism*, Kovach and Rosenstiel make a distinction between two kinds of truth: correspondence and coherence. "For journalism, these tests roughly translate into getting the facts straight and making sense of the facts." They call for a "journalism of verification" to replace a "journalism of assertion:" "A more conscious discipline of verification is the best antidote to being overrun by a new journalism of assertion."

Fairness and objectivity should be regarded as tools to that end, they maintain, rather than as ends in themselves.

One further problem is that the he-said, she-said format is increasingly the best that a reporter can do under the severe time pressure of being required to file continuous updates for a website.

In an article in *The New Yorker* entitled "Non-Stop News," Ken Auletta quoted reporters and press secretaries on what it means to have to feed the Web without being able to take the time to report or even think. "Instead of seeking context or disputing a claim," Auletta writes, "reporters often simply get two opposing quotes and file a he said/she said story."

The Journalism of Assertion

I would like to conclude these reflections with a case study in what I regard as the perils of the journalism of assertion, as practiced by our finest newspaper. Over the last few years, the name David B. Rivkin started showing up in the columns of the *New York Times*. From the manner in which he was quoted in articles relating to various sub-topics concerning the "war on terror," Mr. Rivkin appeared to be an expert on just about any development for which the [George W.] Bush administration needed defending—or for which a federal judge who ruled against the White House needed a thrashing.

For example, in August 2006, when a federal district judge in Detroit declared that the administration's warrantless wiretapping program was unconstitutional, Mr. Rivkin had this to say in the *New York Times* account of the decision: "It is an appallingly bad opinion, bad from both a philosophical and technical perspective, manifesting strong bias."

Mr. Rivkin was identified in the article as "an official in the administrations of President Ronald Reagan and the first President [George H.W.] Bush."

There was no indication of what might have given him the "philosophical perspective" to criticize this court decision so forcefully, or of what evidence he possessed of "strong bias" on the part of the judge, Anna Diggs Taylor. When another judge ruled that some prisoners held by the United States at the Bagram air force base in Afghanistan had the right to petition for *habeas corpus* [freedom from unlawful detention] there was Mr. Rivkin again. He warned that the ruling "gravely undermined" the country's "ability to detain enemy combatants for the duration of hostilities worldwide."

This time he was identified as "an associate White House counsel in the administration of the first President Bush." Since that administration had ended 18 years earlier, I found myself wondering what current expertise Mr. Rivkin possessed that led him to make such a harsh assessment of this new decision.

A check of the *Times* database reveals that since 2006, Mr. Rivkin has been quoted at least 31 times in articles concerning the detainees at Guantanamo Bay (12 times); detainees at Bagram; executive privilege and presidential authority; targeted killing; Iraq; Abu Ghraib; the performance of Attorney General [Michael] Mukasey; and the Central Intelligence Agency and its interrogation policies.

The descriptions of his role and his implied expertise varied from story to story, but the quote was always to the same effect: a strong defense of President Bush and his policies.

The Issue of Expertise

To the extent that David Rivkin has any relevant expertise, the basis for it is not disclosed on his law firm's web site, which contains a full-page biography. He is a partner in the international law firm of Baker Hostetler, identified as a "member of the firm's litigation, international and environmental groups."

The entry describes him as having "in-depth experience with various constitutional issues that are frequently implicated by federal regulatory statutes, including commerce clause-, appointments clause-, and due process-related issues, as well as First and Tenth Amendment-related matters."

He has "extensive experience in international arbitration and policy advocacy on a wide range of international and domestic issues, including treaty implementation, multilateral and unilateral sanctions, corporate law, environmental and energy matters (with an emphasis on policy, regulatory and enforcement issues.)"

His qualifications for practicing law in these areas are evident: during his federal government service in the Reagan and first Bush administrations, he worked on domestic regulatory issues, with a specialty in oil and natural gas. He worked in the Office of Policy Development in the Justice Department and worked for Vice President Bush as legal adviser to the Counsel to the President, later becoming special assistant for domestic policy to Vice President Dan Quayle and associate general counsel in the Department of Energy.

The more I read, the more mystified I became. An article on the prospect that President Obama might transfer some Guantanamo detainees to the United States included a warning from Mr. Rivkin that classified information might be made public during trials in civilian courts—"a danger that David B. Rivkin, an official in the Reagan Justice Department, calls 'the conviction price.'"

When details of the C.I.A.'s [Central Intelligence Agency's] interrogation regime were reported in August, the article contained these sentences: "'Elaborate care went into figuring out the precise gradations of coercion,' said David B. Rivkin Jr., a lawyer who served in the administrations of Ronald Reagan and George H.W. Bush, 'Yes, it's jarring. But it shows how both the lawyers and the nonlawyers tried to do the right thing.'"

An article about President Obama's decision to retain the military commission system for trying detainees at Guantanamo included this:

"David B. Rivkin Jr., a Washington lawyer who was an official in the Reagan administration, said the decision suggested that the Obama administration was coming to accept the Bush administration's thesis that terror suspects should be viewed as enemy fighters, not as criminal defendants with all the rights accorded by American courts. 'I give them great credit for coming to their senses after looking at the dossiers' of the detainees, Mr. Rivkin said."

Articles on Federal Courts

And an article on the prison sentence meted out by a Federal District Judge to a man who admitted having trained with and offering his services to Al Qaeda offered the critique from David Rivkin that the Obama administration should have used a military commission instead of sending the defendant, Al-Marri, to federal court.

There is another side to that story—one that calls on journalists to do their best to provide not just the facts, but also—always—the truth.

The federal courts are "a crapshoot," he said, while military commissions "arrive at a better judgment, being comprised of warriors. . . ." Mr. Rivkin was described in this article as "a lawyer who served in the administrations of President Reagan and the first President Bush.". . .

I find it particularly troubling to use Mr. Rivkin to criticize federal court decisions. When a federal district judge issues a decision, there is no "other side" to the story—the decision is the decision. The "other side" is contained in the briefs presenting the argument that the judge rejected. But digging up the briefs, reading them, and summarizing them takes more work that accepting an *ad hominem* [personal attack] sound bite from someone willing to answer any call.

I actually don't mean to be critical of David Rivkin, a man with whom I have a perfectly pleasant personal relationship.

As a surrogate, a "go-to proxy," he is simply filling a role assigned to him by reporters and—let's assume—editors who accept unquestionably the notion that every story has another side that it is journalism's duty to present. I hope I have persuaded you ... that there is another side to that story—one that calls on journalists to do their best to provide not just the facts, but also—always—the truth.

The Pursuit of Truth Does Not Justify Disclosure of Confidential Information

Victor Davis Hanson

Victor Davis Hanson is the Martin and Illie Anderson Senior Fellow at Stanford University's Hoover Institution, a military historian, and an author.

Julian Assange, the public face of WikiLeaks, is, among many things, cowardly. Courageousness would involve meeting with Iranian dissidents, Russian journalists, Pakistani Christians, or Chinese human-rights activists—and then releasing any confidential information that they might have about the torment institutionalized by their countries' authoritarian regimes. That would be risky to Assange, however, since such governments do not customarily go to court against their leakers; they gulag them—or liquidate them.

So, instead, Assange navigates through the European northwest among the good-life elites whose economic and security protocols he does so much to undermine. Being summoned to a trumped-up Swedish hearing for being an exploitative cad who fails to wear a condom in his ephemeral hook-ups is not the same thing as being dragged into the basement of the Pakistani intelligence service or appearing in an orange jumpsuit on an al-Qaeda execution video. Why does not the peripatetic Assange at least drive about, say, the back roads of the Middle East, Mexico, or Central Africa in his quest for conduits to spread cosmic truth and justice?

A Lack of Principles

In truth, Assange is a sorry product of the postmodern West. He reminds us of the morality of Western shock artists who freely caricature Christianity on the hallowed principle of free speech, but, in a nano-second, censor themselves when Islam might provide an even larger target for their cynical secular disdain. WikiLeaks is the journalistic equivalent of a *Piss Christ* [a controversial photograph] exhibition of the contemporary art world—a repellent reminder of the cowardly selectivity of the shock-jock huckster.

When reminded that his recklessness will lead to violence, mayhem, and deaths, [Assange] dismisses such dangers as insignificant in comparison to the benevolence that he bestows.

Julian Assange is without principles. He seems to think leaking confidential communications proves that the vast right-wing military-industrial-financial complex is harming either the most affluent, free Western population in the history of civilization or the globalized world itself—one that has done more to eliminate poverty and extend freedom in the last two decades than had been done at any other time in recorded history. We know from Climategate that the world's green scientists are every bit as conniving, petty, and mean-spirited as any American diplomat. I would like to see the secret communications that buzz back and forth among Hollywood agents, producers, and financiers to learn of the real criteria that led to box-office bombs like *Redacted* and *Rendition* being written, cast, financed, and made. Maybe to calibrate the level of sincerity and honesty among our movers and shakers, we can read the minutes of Harvard or Yale tenure committees, some correspondence from the minions of [Hungarian-American investor and philanthropist] George Soros, or the communications of the [United Nations] U.N.

secretary general—or, better yet, the encrypted e-mail transcripts of exchanges among the WikiLeaks board. Apparently Assange thinks that confidentiality is trafficked only among the suspicious Western ruling classes, while dissidents like himself are fueled instead by "truth." But if a man cannot be honest with a woman during intimacy, what can he be honest about?—whoops, one should not rush to an Assange-like judgment on the basis of gossip and innuendo; one should wait until the suspicious personage has had his day in court.

Transparency and Honesty

So Julian Assange is also a juvenile. Like some warmed-over let-it-all-hang-out Sixties loudmouth, he seems to think that transparency to the fullest is honesty, without a clue that truth is the final product that emerges from a combination of self-reflection, self-doubt, and introspection. These diplomatic cables contain raw gossip, half-baked impressions, innuendos, self-serving snideness, trial balloons, and witticisms among supposedly sober and judicious diplomats. Yet entering such confidential conversations *in mediis rebus* [in the middle of things] short-circuits, rather than enhances, the truth. In the adult world, venting to others does not necessarily translate into duplicity; actions are often a better indicator of veracity than rumblings and musings. Only a perpetual adolescent believes that one has to be perfect in word and thought to be good. The United States no doubt is told all the time by preening Gulf sheiks to hit Iran, but that does not mean that we or even they wish to reify such braggadocio. So far the real truth is our actions, which suggest that we do not think it is wise to bomb Iran.

Julian Assange is a narcissist. Like all self-absorbed egos who deny their selfishness, he protests that he wished WikiLeaks to remain an anonymously run, collective effort—while he ensured that it most certainly would not be, as he jetted the globe, giving dozens of media interviews, leveling threats, pontificating about world leaders who should resign, and promising to drop embarrassing megatonnage of gossip should he, Julian Assange, ever be charged.

The Impact of Government Disclosures

Julian Assange has more or less ensured that WikiLeaks would be synonymous with Julian Assange and that he would be its man-of-the-year face on *Time* magazine. Like all narcissists, when reminded that his recklessness will lead to violence, mayhem, and deaths, he dismisses such dangers as insignificant in comparison to the benevolence that he bestows. Note how easily a computer hacker with a criminal record has established himself as judge, jury, and executioner on behalf of world truth. When he says, "I have become a lightning rod," he means, "I am the [flamboyant singer/entertainer] Lady Gaga of leaking."

His one mistake? Assange unfortunately got his sweepstakes trove from [US Army soldier] Bradley Manning during the [Barack] Obama administration. Up until then, the global liberal media culture had less of a problem with WikiLeaks, since government disclosures only confirmed the nefarious nature of reactionaries like George W. Bush. But now in the age of progressive governance, we are learning that Secretary [Hillary] Clinton spies, that President Obama's diplomats are jaded and cynical, and that such disclosures have hurt the presidency of a liberal progressive. It is one thing to canonize a Daniel Ellsberg [former US military analyst who released the Pentagon Papers] or transmogrify the serial deceiver [former US diplomat] Joe Wilson into a victim of Dick Cheney's dark plots, but quite another to deify a leaker whose machinations will serve to undermine the agenda of Barack Obama. To paraphrase [English author and journalist] George Orwell, Assange is learning that all leaks are essential—but some leaks are more essential than others.

Undercover Reporting Is Not Always Justified and Should Be Used Sparingly

Greg Marx

Greg Marx is a student at the Columbia University Graduate School of Journalism and staff writer for the Columbia Journalism Review.

When news broke in late January [2010] that James O'Keefe and three other men, two of whom were costumed as telephone repairmen, had been arrested by federal authorities and charged with "interfering" with the phone system at the New Orleans office of Sen. Mary Landrieu, observers of all sorts shared a similar response: What were they thinking?

Tactics with a History

Thanks to a statement O'Keefe has posted at Andrew Breitbart's BigGovernment.com and an interview he gave Monday night to Fox News's Sean Hannity, we now have a pretty good answer to that question. Landrieu had drawn the ire of some conservatives for her participation in a deal that helped advance health care reform, and the anger had grown amid claims that her office was avoiding calls from constituents. O'Keefe told Hannity:

> We wanted to get to the bottom of the claim that [Landrieu] was not answering her phones, her phones were jammed. We wanted to find out why her constituents couldn't get through to her. We wanted to verify the reports.

And while O'Keefe has acknowledged that, "on reflection, I could have used a different approach to this investigation," he also told Hannity he was operating in an established tradition: "We used the same tactics that investigative journalists have been using. In all the videos I do, I pose as something I'm not to try to get to the bottom of the truth." During the interview, he and Hannity name-checked a few specific predecessors, among them *PrimeTime Live*'s Food Lion investigation, *60 Minutes, 20/20*, and *Dateline NBC*, including its "To Catch a Predator" series.

Considering the extent to which O'Keefe's activities are driven by political goals, it's debatable whether or not he really belongs to this family tree. But even taking him at his word, lumping O'Keefe in with those programs doesn't necessarily put him on the safe ground he's looking for. Journalism ethicists have long been wary of deceptive undercover tactics that those programs (and others) use—and with good reason. Overreliance on sting operations and subterfuge can weaken the public's trust in the media and compromise journalists' claim to be truth-tellers. Undercover reporting can be a powerful tool, but it's one to be used cautiously: against only the most important targets, and even then only when accompanied by solid traditional reporting.

While the use of deception in reporting can yield sensational results, it also lends the subject a weapon to wield against the journalist.

Wariness About Undercover Reporting

The field's squeamishness with "lying to get the truth," as the headline of a 2007 *American Journalism Review* article put it, is well-documented. In the 1970s, the *Chicago Sun-Times* set up an elaborate sting operation at the Mirage Tavern to document routine corruption in city agencies; the sting worked, but the paper's Pulitzer hopes were dashed, reportedly because Ben Bradlee and Eugene Patterson disapproved of its methods. *PrimeTime Live*'s decision to have producers falsify resumes and smuggle hidden cameras into a Food Lion grocery store sparked contentious litigation (an initial $5.5 million jury verdict against ABC was reduced on appeal to $2) and drew two articles in *CJR* [*Columbia Journalism Review*].

> *While the use of deception in reporting can yield sensational results, it also lends the subject a weapon to wield against the journalist.*

Most recently, Ken Silverstein, the acclaimed Washington editor of *Harper's*, posed as a foreign businessman to expose lobbyists' willingness to represent unsavory clients. Silverstein came back with a gripping story and had plenty of defenders, but institutions like the Center for Public Integrity sided with *The Washington Post*'s Howard Kurtz in criticizing his methods.

In other words, press criticism of O'Keefe may reflect ideological disagreement in some cases. More broadly, it no doubt reflects some *schadenfreude* [happiness in another's misfortune] from an institution he and his patron Breitbart have conspicuously disdained. But it's also consistent with the wariness with which much of the media—especially the print media—has long viewed undercover reporting.

Fallout from the Use of Deception

There are practical reasons for that wariness. As other observers have noted, while the use of deception in reporting can yield sensational results, it also lends the subject a weapon to wield against the journalist. The ready-made complaint: If the reporter has forfeited the high ground of transparency and honesty, how can his conclusions be trusted by the public? The fallout may not be limited to the case at hand. During the

Food Lion controversy, Marvin Kalb of Harvard's Shorenstein Center worried that widespread use of deception "demeans journalism and damages badly the journalist and the public." (This is not a theoretical problem. In announcing the verdict in the Food Lion case, the jury foreman told ABC, "You didn't have boundaries when you started this investigation.... You kept pushing on the edges and pushing on the edges.... It was too extensive and fraudulent.")

To mitigate this concern, undercover reporters are urged [to] take care to situate what they've gleaned through deception in a structure of traditional reporting—to show that, unlike, say, [TV shows] *Punk'd* or *Candid Camera* or even "To Catch a Predator," the gimmick is not all there is. Wherever one comes down on Silverstein's work, one of the more effective criticisms of it was that his original story never gave the lobbying firms he targeted an opportunity to comment. A similar criticism applies to O'Keefe's ACORN [Association of Community Organizations for Reform Now] videos, which made him a national figure—whatever malfeasance he may have uncovered at ACORN, his failure to present his videos in any broader reportorial context made it difficult for the national media to take his allegations seriously. (And when other journalists did look into the story, they found that the footage, while containing some truly troubling material, should not all be taken at face value.)

Guidelines for Undercover Reporting

That's not the only guideline for going undercover. While there are, appropriately, no hard-and-fast rules or central authorities for journalism, a checklist drawn up by Poynter's [Poynter Institute's] Bob Steele in 1995 is often cited for guidance on this issue. A few points on the list are probably too vague to be of much use, but the first two are valuable. They state that deception and hidden cameras may be appropriate:

When the information obtained is of profound importance. It must be of vital public interest, such as revealing great "system failure" at the top levels, or it must prevent profound harm to individuals.

When all other alternatives for obtaining the same information have been exhausted.

Whether something is of "profound importance" is obviously a matter of news judgment, but there's good reason to question O'Keefe's. If his focus on ACORN was the product of a worldview that vastly exaggerated that group's practical political importance, his decision that Landrieu's phone system merited a hidden-camera investigation was even more off the mark.

Public officials should be responsive to their constituents, and when credible concerns are raised that they aren't, the press should check them out. But even if O'Keefe's suspicions about Landrieu turned out to be true, her actions would count as little more than a good-government misdemeanor. Deciding that they warranted undercover treatment is a reflection of editorial judgment unconstrained by common sense.

Of course, O'Keefe's comment to Hannity—"In all the videos I do, I pose as something I'm not"—suggests that he skipped this balancing test entirely. Attempts to reach O'Keefe for comment were unsuccessful, but in an interview late Wednesday night [February 3, 2010] Breitbart defended his approach. "My tactics are unorthodox, and his tactics are unorthodox, because the mainstream media is full of shit," he said. "When we report the truth, you ignore it." Later, he added, "You guys are creating the market for creative journalism,—it wouldn't be there if you guys did your job." (Whatever the merits of this argument, it is not exactly the defense that O'Keefe has advanced.)

All this may seem like so much legalistic hair-splitting to readers and viewers; in the big picture whether O'Keefe's work is best thought of as "journalism," "activism," or something else may be a niche concern. But as long as he's trying to claim the mantle of undercover reporting, it's worth noting that that tradition is more complicated, and more contested, than he's acknowledging.

Journalists Should Be Careful in Deciding What Becomes News

Stephen J.A. Ward

Stephen J.A. Ward is the James E. Burgess Professor of Journalism Ethics in the School of Journalism and Mass Communication at the University of Wisconsin-Madison, and director of the school's Center for Journalism Ethics.

As America approached, nervously and disunited, the ninth anniversary of the 9/11 [2001] terrorist attack, the pastor of a small Florida church bathed in a global media spotlight.

Rev. Terry Jones and his small Dove World Outreach Center had announced in July [2010] their plan to burn copies of the Koran to proclaim the evil of Islam. By September, the pastor's unholy plan was top of the news around the world, sparking riots and prompting widespread criticism.

On one day alone, Jones's blatant media manipulation garnered front page coverage in over 50 USA daily papers. Moderate Christians and Muslims can only dream of such widespread coverage of their ideas.

Blatant Media Manipulation

The questions asked repeatedly on media programs were: "How did this little-known pastor get so much news coverage? Should the media have given him a global platform for his questionable views and potentially harmful actions?"

Let's ask a larger question: How does any story become top of the news? How is news selected? Media scholars have itemized many factors, such as: the event's novel or dramatic

Stephen J.A. Ward, "Terry Jones Syndrome: Guidelines for Responsible News Selection," Center for Journalism Ethics, September 21, 2010. http:ethics.journalism.wisc.edu.

nature; involvement of prominent people; cost of doing the story; editor's judgments about what is interesting for readers; and whether the story connects with larger trends.

There is an ethical side to news selection.

To this list we can add two relatively new factors: creation of a global media world inhabited by countless online websites, bloggers, and commentators; and the existence of many political groups that will use this global media to attack opponents and provoke riots.

Many of these factors elevated the Koran-burning plan to global status.

Responsible News Selection

Besides these facts, there is an ethical side to news selection: What events should receive extensive coverage? What guidelines can help newsrooms respond responsibly to a Terry Jones and a soon-to-follow host of copycats?

In the Jones story, the question of responsible news selection must consider two different time periods: In the summer, when the plan was first announced; and in late August, when the story had gone viral. In the early weeks, newsrooms should have ignored Jones's plan. And there was no justification for selecting Jones's announcement as an important news story. At the very most, the announcement merited an initial item on the controversial pastor from Gainesville, Florida. However, the decision to run a small, initial item needs to be balanced against the fear that even modest coverage might spark a global reaction. . . .

But what should responsible editors do when the media system turns the story into an ugly global incident, with leaders predicting that a Koran burning would incite violence?

Caught inside this media maelstrom, responsible editors cannot ignore the story. So, what guidelines can help the beleaguered editor who resents giving Jones more publicity?

Principles for News Selection

There are no easy answers. Yet editors can consult the following principles:

Democracy needs intelligent news selection. A democracy whose media is distracted by sensational events is headed for trouble. A media that does not—or will not—distinguish between trivial and essential news, or between genuine news makers and media manipulators, creates a society that is under-informed on the crucial issues that define its future.

It is not the job of journalists to provide unthinking coverage of events that are gratuitously manufactured to provoke and cause harm.

Journalists should ask to what degree their news selection is based on a sober assessment of what really is important—developments in the political, economic, legal, and social arenas of the body politic.

When a Terry Jones gets too much air time, or when [socialite] Paris Hilton's latest faux pas trends on Twitter—and the blogosphere is abuzz—this is exactly the time when journalists must push back in the opposite direction. They must question a news selection that feeds this media circus. Of course, media should cover pop culture and the merely novel; but the media's news selection should not be hostage to alleged news events or entertainment values.

Go hard on manipulators. News selection should be guided by who is seeking media attention and why. Jones guessed correctly that a book burning would get attention. He loved appearing before the cameras and toying with reporters. Editors have every right to work against a manipulator's media strategy. It is not the job of journalists to provide unthinking coverage of events that are gratuitously manufactured to provoke and cause harm.

Swim against the flow by doing good journalism. Even if a story is too big to ignore, journalists and newsrooms are not helpless victims of a faceless "media world." They can do three things when confronted by a Terry Jones.

Practice proportionality: avoid the drama: Reduce the quantity of coverage and reduce the prominence of the story. For example, in the lead up to Sept. 11, the Associated Press announced that it would reduce the number of stories it would do on the Jones affair, and would not distribute images or audio that specifically showed Korans being burned.

Relentlessly provide context: Widen the story by avoiding a narrow focus on the event in question. For example, in the case of Jones, do not follow his every move. Also, explain who Jones is and the size of his church. Note his previous attempts to get media attention and question whether his views are affirmed by many Americans. On a number of days, the *New York Times* reduced the impact of the Jones story by folding the event into larger explanatory stories of how Americans were approaching the 9/11 anniversary.

Be a catalyst for informed discussion: Deepen a story like the Jones plan by including other voices, such as moderate Muslim leaders and interfaith associations that are rallying against Jones. Use this moment to bring intolerant views about Islam out into the open for rigorous review. Rather than try to pretend that people like Jones don't exist, use this shabby affair as an opportunity to spark a more reasoned and intelligent discussion of religion. Meet intolerant, uninformed speech with tolerant, informed speech.

Are these principles of responsible news selection too old fashioned to operate in a world of global media and instantaneous online commentary? They better not be. Our pluralistic democracies will be neither informed nor peaceful unless a core of journalists and newsrooms remain committed to responsible news selection.

In a media-linked world, this is no time for journalists to play follow the leader—or follow the most irresponsible.

I say, let's follow our principles.

Chapter 3

Should Journalists Avoid Actions That Compromise Objectivity?

Overview: Objectivity in the New Era

Joe Strupp

Joe Strupp is an investigative reporter and senior editor at Media Matters for America, a progressive media watchdog information center.

When Michael Paulson began covering religion for *The Boston Globe* eight years ago [2000], the paper had no blogs or online video, he did almost no outside speaking work, and the paper's Pulitzer Prize-winning coverage of the Catholic church sex scandal was still years away. Today, Paulson finds himself going well beyond the straight news stories of the print edition—to more analysis, public speaking and commentary, and, in just the past few months, a religion-focused blog.

New Journalistic Challenges

He's not alone. While Paulson, 43, contends the objective approach to reporting is maintained on all fronts, he says that keeping up in so many journalistic outlets can be difficult: "There is a difference between being analytical and being opinionated. A blog is much more challenging because it is first-person. It is very fast, and in the world of blogging, most bloggers are offering opinions all the time. When newspapers add the format of blogging, I am not allowed the leeway of the traditional blogger."

Paulson's challenge is one that more and more print journalists are confronting as they are asked to write news stories, blog items, do analysis (often minutes after an event has occurred) and, in many cases, provide commentary for radio, television, and even online outlets. As newspaper Web sites blend in more with blogs that do not hold to the same journalistic rules, there is greater pressure to "write like them"— and sometimes cut corners on the principles of objectivity and balance that have been the oft-stated mainstay, for better or worse, of newspaper news coverage.

"I see a lot of cheering in the press box that used to not be the way," says Carla Marinucci, a 12-year political reporter for the *San Francisco Chronicle* who noted a much more partisan tone at this year's political conventions due to many bloggers in attendance than in the past. "All of us have to be very careful in this brave new world—a lot of places are calling for your opinion."

Paulson's boss, *Globe* Editor Martin Baron, agrees that the challenges are greater, but stresses that is no excuse for newspapers getting away from the core demands of journalism: "We need to be honest, accurate and fair. Those are the principles. Those are the words that define what our mission is. The others send us in odd directions." But, he adds, "that doesn't mean a blog cannot have a personality or be more casual or irreverent in certain ways. It has a certain style to it, much like a feature has a different style to it. But it is still grounded by core principles."

The Goal of Objectivity

Others claim the reporter's rule of remaining objective has never really been the case, and for newspapers to pretend to "hold on" to it in the growing age of online opinions and fast-moving facts only holds them back. "I'm not a believer in the myth of objectivity to begin with—what we are talking about is fairness," says Keith Woods, dean of faculty at the Poynter Institute. "We may aspire to [objectivity], but we have not come close to achieving it."

Woods explains that as reporters move into new areas, it becomes much harder to keep your opinions to yourself as you move across forms. "Invariably, one leaks into another. Writing a blog, then going on radio or TV to give an opinion, then writing a staff news story is more difficult."

Some newspaper stalwarts . . . say such a mixed bag of media these days requires reporters to keep to the core journalistic standards more than ever.

He points to the changes in media for readers, who just 10 or 20 years ago had much less opinion-driven content from which to select. Even CNN, which launched more than 25 years ago, has taken a decidedly more personality-driven and opinionated tone, something on display even more so at somewhat newer competitors like MSNBC. When a viewer of those channels turns to a newspaper, in print or online, they may be expecting a slanted viewpoint—and sometimes want one.

"I have given up watching CNN to try to determine who is a pundit and who is a journalist," says Woods. "The public no longer sees the printed page as the only domain of the journalist. They are in all of these forms. Too often now, opinion is substituted as fact, and the collection of opinion is substituted for reporting."

The Standards for Newspapers

But some newspaper stalwarts like John Walcott, McClatchy Newspapers' Washington bureau chief, say such a mixed bag of media these days requires reporters to keep to the core journalistic standards more than ever. "The process is well under way, lumping all of us together," he says of the public's perception of the media. "We have to keep our standards as high as we can."

He adds, however, that the new forms such as blogs and video and analysis are necessary, and his site has launched numerous such options in the past few years. "They all have fairly strict guidelines" on keeping personal opinion out of the mix, he says of the blogs, many of which emanate from foreign bureaus. "Once you cross the line, there is no easy way to cross back."

The *Chronicle*'s Marinucci says she already sees the impact non-newspaper outlets have had on public perception, noting numerous instances in which she is accused of slanting one way or another, much more than even a few years ago. She cites a blog post in early 2008 about John Edwards, long outspoken about poverty, accepting $50,000 to speak at a college campus on the issue. "I got very nasty, obscene e-mails, supposedly from Edwards supporters," she says. "Even though I kept my opinion out of it."

The growing trend is that the truth must surpass the 50/50 doctrine.

Andrew Malcolm, who has covered politics since 1968 and blogs at the *Los Angeles Times*' "Top of the Ticket," says he still treats each item like a fact-based story, but with some buzz and style. "Most non-newspaper blogs are committed, one way or another—there is a slant," he says. "They are selling a particular view. Our niche is to be sort of unexpected. But it is possible to be a real professional. Cover something straight and develop a perspective to inform your discussion."

The 50/50 Doctrine

L.A. Times Washington bureau chief Doyle McManus points out the different views of what is objective. "I think it means presenting every side of an argument fairly in ways that the proponents would accept as valid," he says.

But more and more, both new media and old-fashioned news types are disagreeing with that approach. The growing trend is that the truth must surpass the 50/50 doctrine. "We have gotten it so wrong with the idea of giving equal play to both sides," says Arianna Huffington, editor-in-chief of Huffingtonpost.com and a longtime proponent of trading arbitrary "balance" for truth. "We are not always going to be balanced. Very often, it is one side or the other." She cited the ongoing arguments against global warming, which she contends mainstream journalists allowed for too long to go unchallenged: "We wasted a lot of journalistic capital on global warming trying to be balanced." She says the recent government rescue of financial institutions is another, noting too many mainstream outlets did not question if the bailout was needed: "Those of us who live online already dismissed certain elements of the bailout, such as the lack of oversight."

Adds Woods at Poynter: "Whether you quote both sides does not change what is the truth. We allow the 50/50 idea to substitute for truth. Where we often fail is when we may get somebody on one side with deep knowledge, understanding, perspective, and credibility to speak and on the other side someone with just an opinion, but they have no credibility."

Baron at the *Globe* agrees: "We are involved in journalism, not stenography exercises. It is finding out what is actually happening. Balance means every story gets 50/50? I don't believe that."

Hidden Political Contributions by Journalists Destroys Credibility

Kevin Smith

Kevin Smith is the ethics committee chairman for the Society of Professional Journalists.

Tuesday night [November 9, 2010] MSNBC commentator Keith Olbermann spent the last five minutes of his show issuing apologies for the furor that erupted last week when it was revealed he had made political contributions to three congressional candidates.

For his action MSNBC execs, citing ethical guidelines, suspended him for two shows, and America was forced to live through another example of journalism gone wrong.

So, there he was Tuesday night, the snarky tone evident in his voice and that jeering look in his eyes as he began his *mea culpa* [acknowledgment of fault].

A Conflict of Interest

He apologized on three fronts. First, for subjecting the audience to the drama (though he seemed to relish the fact he had more than 300,000 people sign a petition supporting his actions); second, for not knowing "by observation" there was company policies against political contributions without prior notification to superiors (he said he thinks it's completely illegal to have such mandates); and finally, for not revealing a contribution to his audience the next day when he slapped Arizona Republican congressional candidate Jesse Kelly in his "Worst Person" segment. Kelly's opposition was Democratic candidate Gabrielle Giffords, a $2,400 donor recipient. His other $2,400 benefactors included candidates Jack Conway in Kentucky and Raul Grijalva, also of Arizona.

But, what I never heard was an apology for the donations themselves. There was nothing to suggest that Olbermann thinks there was anything wrong with a journalist giving money to politician candidates. He dodged apologizing for the basis of the problem. In fact, he went in the opposite direction saying he thinks the donation rules "need to be adjusted to adapt to the realities of 21st century journalism."

Olbermann just doesn't get it.

Where once uniform credibility meant everything to a journalist, many are gladly opting now for "niche" or "community" credibility among like mentalities.

He can snarl and flash those leering looks into the camera all he wants, and he can have colleagues point accusatory fingers at Fox News on his behalf, but the bottom line is clear: His obvious conflict of interest and his forfeiture of independence doesn't register with him nor the legions of supporters, some journalists themselves, who think that taking overtly subjective stands and advancing those causes is the "reality of 21st century journalism."

A Decline in Uniform Credibility

Olbermann used to cover sports, so maybe this analogy helps. Think Pete Rose betting on baseball games. Both men placed money in a gamble to achieve a desired outcome, one that ultimately benefits their interests and careers. Olbermann hopes that by his donation he can help create Democratic victories, something that certainly stands to benefit his program that relies on a steady feast off the liberal carcass. In the end they both wanted to alter the outcomes in a way that benefitted them. Both represent corruption of the profession.

So we are led to believe by Olbermann's assessment there is a new age in 21st century journalism that tosses aside reliable tenets of fairness and honesty in reporting. That this new age can turn its back on independence and disclosure of conflicts and that "partial" journalists who deal in commentary get to live by a different set of rules than "impartial" journalists (most everyone else who doesn't work for MSNBC or Fox).

That we are separating journalists into subcategories of "partial" and "impartial" as I've seen touted by bloggers means American journalism is hosting a growing ethical sideshow. Where once uniform credibility meant everything to a journalist, many are gladly opting now for "niche" or "community" credibility among like mentalities.

Niche credibility translated means I report whatever I want, say whatever I want, alter the facts and reality however I want and tear down the foundations of ethical journalism if they become an obstruction. In the end, as long as I have credibility within my select audience or community, then that's what stands for responsible journalism.

The Ethical Foundations of Journalism

When Plato put forth the notion of communitarianism as an ethic foundation, one that puts community values and development first over individual morals, it's a safe bet that he wasn't supporting the notion of rouge communities springing up within a greater society, each with their own set of standards that would repeal the overarching values of society as a whole. And it's doubtful he'd advocate for journalism's ethical foundations to be pared into subsets depending on how you chose to practice the craft or the medium you resort to.

For now, Olbermann and his minions don't get to stratify ethics based on titles and television ratings. They'll have to follow the standards most journalists do in developing that sacred trust with the public. And that's a trust you can't put a price on, though we know now you can lose it for $2,400.

Journalists Should Not Make Predictions in Reporting the News

Glenn Greenwald

Glenn Greenwald is a columnist for Salon *and the author of* With Liberty and Justice for Some: How the Law Is Used to Destroy Equality and Protect the Powerful.

The record of the American pundit class with regard to the 2008 presidential election can be summarized in one word: wrong. For the last twelve months [April 2007 to April 2008] political journalists in unison have created and then imposed countless predictive narratives onto their "news" coverage of the campaign, narratives which have repeatedly turned out to be completely inaccurate. Yet they never learn their lesson, are never held accountable and virtually never acknowledge their errors. Political punditry is the ultimate accountability-free profession.

The Media's Coverage of Campaigns

It is not merely opinionists who have spun these predictive tales, but so-called straight reporters as well. Indeed, dominating the media's news coverage of presidential campaigns are claims about what is likely to happen in the future. Rather than focusing on the candidates' records, the validity of their positions or the truth of their factual assertions, political election coverage instead is obsessed primarily with the question of who is likely to win and lose. Like most fortune-tellers, reporters' fixation on predictive narratives has left a virtually unbroken string of humiliating errors.

Throughout all of 2007, without a single vote having been cast, two themes dominated the media's coverage of the race. First, Hillary Clinton's nomination was essentially inevitable; her lead in the polls was insurmountable, and her organizational strength rendered her invulnerable to any challenges. Second, John McCain's candidacy was over, killed by campaign mismanagement, conservative anger over his immigration stance, independent resentment over his support for the "surge," a lack of funds and Rudy Giuliani's bulging popular lead.

It is little wonder that reporters are so woefully inept at predicting the voting behavior of people with whom they have virtually nothing in common.

Yet suddenly, by the end of January 2008, after just a few weeks of voting in a handful of small states, Barack Obama and John McCain were declared to be the all-but-certain nominees. Hillary Clinton and Rudy Giuliani were but failed afterthoughts. Within a matter of a few short weeks, the year-long pundit script was instantaneously rewritten—just scrapped—with barely any acknowledgment that it ever existed.

The Vast Gap

Coddled, well-compensated national journalists view elections as a fun game—something about which they gossip with one another, constantly reinforcing their own groupthink biases—but not as anything that truly matters. By stark contrast, the average voter, faced with increasing economic insecurity and concerns over a whole variety of pressing problems, actually believes that important matters are at stake, that the outcome of elections can profoundly affect their futures and their families. It is little wonder that reporters are so woefully inept at predicting the voting behavior of people with whom they have virtually nothing in common.

The vast gap between the prevailing journalistic narrative and reality has extended to virtually every predictive story line, large and small, and encompasses everything from foreign- and domestic-policy debates to national elections. A favorite tactic with virtually every pundit is to take whatever their own personal opinion happens to be, preface it with the phrase "Americans believe" or "most Americans think," and then appoint themselves Spokesman for the American People. Even worse, while they cast themselves as the mouthpiece of the Silent, Noble American Majority, it just so happens that "Americans" now overwhelmingly reject their belief system.

An Example of Speaking for the People

Mr. David Brooks of the *New York Times* is an especially prominent pundit who favors this tactic. In one such moment where he channeled the voice of the "American People," Brooks proclaimed that their greatest hope was to continue to rule the world—and particularly the Middle East—with the United States' mighty, dominant military power.

> Americans are having a debate about how to proceed in Iraq, but we are not having a strategic debate about retracting American power and influence. What's most important about this debate is what doesn't need to be said. No major American leader doubts that America must remain, as Dean Acheson put it, the locomotive of the world. . . .
>
> This is not a country looking to avoid entangling alliances. This is not a country renouncing the threat of force. This is not a country looking to come home again. The Iraq syndrome is over before it even had a chance to begin.

So, according to Brooks, this is just "another chapter in [America's] long expansionist story." And think twice if you presume the Iraq experience is going to prevent a U.S. attack on Iran. Americans still crave the "dominant role in the world."

But let us not be fooled into thinking he really speaks for the American people. Oddly enough, there's a way to find out.

It's called "polling data." I can happily point out that we hear nary a whisper of these facts in Brooks's piece and his oft-repeated claims about what Americans think are purely false. Neoconservative fantasies aside, military adventures are increasingly repudiated by Americans. A Pew poll of early February 2006 states:

> When President Bush delivered a strong warning against isolationism in Tuesday's State of the Union address, he was speaking to a recent and dramatic turn in public opinion. A recent Pew Research survey found a decided revival of isolationist sentiment among the public, to levels not seen since [the] post-Cold War 1990s and the post-Vietnam 1970s. Moreover, one of the main pillars of Bush's argument in favor of global engagement—the need to promote democracy around the world—has not struck a chord with the public. Support for that objective has been consistently tepid, even among members of Bush's own party.

Particularly, the idea that the United States should topple foreign governments and "spread freedom" is pretty much as marginalized as you can get:

> Of thirteen foreign policy priorities tested in Pew's October [2005] survey, "promoting democracy in other nations" came in dead last. . . . And in contrast with public opinion on most foreign policy questions these days, there is no partisan divide—Republicans and Democrats agree. . . .

Opinion Masquerading as News

We see an offshoot of this phenomenon with the venerable Howard Kurtz of CNN/*Washington Post*, who has a tendency to recycle stories from the right-wing blogosphere, passing them off as what America needs to know. With what seems to be a little jig, he recites the emerging Beltway wisdom that—gasp!—we just might be winning in Iraq. And that just might hurt the Democrats in the election.

But hope against Howard-Kurtz hope, people just don't seem to be changing their minds. Yet again, polling data released a couple of days after Kurtz's article of November 6, 2007, this time from CNN, showed that overall, 68 percent of Americans were opposed to the war in Iraq—a new record. And again devastating to Brooks's point, 63 percent opposed air strikes on Iran. That number jumped up to 73 when we talk about adding ground troops to a military adventure.

But Brooks, Kurtz, the *Politico*'s Jim VandeHei, David Broder and Shailagh Murray at the *Washington Post*, and others still promise that this is all going to work out. Pundits like these love to pretend that they are free of political opinion and bias and instead masquerade as Spokesmen for the People, attributing to those People the views which the pundits themselves harbor but will not acknowledge. Time and again, this self-centered, self-referential method for opining about political matters produces claims and predictions which are dead wrong.

A Prediction by the Press

And these relentlessly inaccurate predictions were unending in the weeks prior to the first nationwide vote, the January 3 Iowa caucus; polls almost unanimously showed an increasingly large lead for the former GOP governor of Arkansas, Mike Huckabee. For months, the press had ignored Huckabee as an irrelevant also-ran, and the surge of support reflected by these polls—coming from the state's large evangelical voter block—was predicted by virtually none of the pundits.

As Huckabee's increased polling strength brought him more media attention, he committed a series of what journalists refer to as "gaffes"—mistakes that, in the eyes of the pundit class, reflected what a terribly unsophisticated candidate he was, a mere "rookie" unfamiliar with the time-tested Beltway rules for how a candidate should behave. Each time Huckabee violated one of their sacred principles, journalists insisted with great certainty that the latest gaffe would harm

Hucakabee's prospects in Iowa. Yet Huckabee's lead continued to grow as a result of the evangelical voters who were completely indifferent to the petty insider mistakes on which the pundit class was so fixated.

The gap between the perceptions of the pundit class and ordinary voters could scarcely be any larger or more self-evident.

Huckabee's most scorn-inducing "mistake" occurred during a late-December press conference held just before the Iowa caucus. He announced his campaign had produced a negative ad aimed at his rival, Mitt Romney, but that he, Huckabee, had insisted it not be used. Nonetheless, Huckabee showed the ad to reporters then and there—a move which journalists covering the Iowa race, with virtual unanimity, condemned as a nakedly cynical and unsophisticated ploy to reap the benefits of quashing a negative ad while, at the same time, ensuring its circulation by showing it to reporters at the press conference.

To the oh-so-knowing national press, this process mistake was not merely embarrassing, but would be fatal to Huckabee's campaign. One after the next—like a flock of birds parroting each other—they pronounced Huckabee's campaign mortally wounded by this grave error.

"That sound you hear rumbling out of Des Moines appears to be a monumental implosion," intoned *Time*'s Joe Klein the next day, in an item he entitled "Huckabust." The *Politico*'s Mike Allen wrote, "The national political press corps ... had a harmonic convergence yesterday on a single point: Huckabee lost it at his news conference yesterday." Allen's *Politico* colleague, Jonathan Martin, echoed, "Huckabee has found himself under the unforgiving glare of the front-runner's spotlight, and his hopes to win here have now become severely threatened by it."

A String of Errors

A mere two days after Huckabee's Iowa media obituary was written, the caucus was held. Huckabee, with 34 percent of the vote, crushed all of his opponents, including the far-better-funded and -organized former governor of Massachusetts, Mitt Romney, and the yearlong front-runner, Rudy Giuliani. What national journalists were so certain was such a significant, even fatal, event—Huckabee's comments about the negative ad—could not have been of any less importance to Iowa voters. The gap between the perceptions of the pundit class and ordinary voters could scarcely be any larger or more self-evident.

Following Iowa, journalists had a new, universally embraced story line: Barack Obama's Iowa win and large polling lead in the next state, New Hampshire, meant that his nomination had become inevitable, while the prior "inevitable" nominee, Hillary Clinton, was now destined to fail. Four days later, Clinton won New Hampshire, and that script, too, was instantly scrapped. In the wake of the New Hampshire press debacle, the *Politico* was one of the very few American news outlets to acknowledge just how continuously wrong the media has been, as John Harris and Jim VandeHei published a candid *mea culpa* [acknowledgment of fault] documenting the press's yearlong string of failures.

The *Politico* duo noted that the loser in New Hampshire was not only Obama but also "us": "'Us' is the community of reporters, pundits and prognosticators who so confidently—and so rashly—stake our reputations on the illusion that we understand politics and have special insight that allows us to predict the behavior of voters." Itemizing the countless number of factually false predictive story lines the American press had manufactured throughout the year, they continued:

> If journalists were candidates, there would be insurmount-able pressure for us to leave the race. If the court of public

opinion were a real court, the best a defense lawyer could do is plea bargain out of a charge that reporters are frauds in exchange for a signed confession that reporters are fools.

The admission of systematic error from Harris and Vande-Hei is notable because of how rare it is. Reporters virtually never acknowledge just how wrong their predictive claims turn out to be. While the New Hampshire error was too blatant to ignore completely—television and print reporters spent days telling their audience that Obama's victory was certain only to watch as Clinton won—most ended up dismissively blaming the pollsters for their mistakes, rather than acknowledging, let alone meaningfully discussing, the fundamental flaws in their coverage that have produced this deeply embarrassing record of wrongness.

Predicting the future is a completely inappropriate role for political reporters to play.

And so we come back again to the Iraq War and more recent wrongheaded predictions. In their never-ending hope that Americans will begin to support the McCain position on Iraq, the *Politico* published a blatantly one-sided article, authored by David Paul Kuhn and citing the now-infamous Michael O'Hanlon of the Brookings Institution:

> The uptick in public support is a promising sign for Republican candidates who have been bludgeoned over the Bush administration's war policies. But no candidate stands to gain more than McCain.

But on the very same day, a *USA Today*/Gallup poll was released, showing—surprise, surprise—that 60 percent of Americans wanted to "set a timetable for removing troops and stick to it regardless of what is going on in Iraq." And that runs pretty much contrary to the McCain position.

An Inappropriate Role

As a general matter, there is no reason whatsoever why report-ers—as opposed to pundits—ought to be infusing predictions into their reporting at all. Predicting the future is a completely inappropriate role for political reporters to play, yet it com-poses virtually the entirety of their election coverage. If one reads *Time* or the *New Republic* or the *Politico* or the *Washing-ton Post*, one is hard-pressed to find any examples of straight-factual reporting about the remaining candidates, their posi-tions, anything substantive—as opposed to endless, groupthink gossip about tactics and campaigns and winning/losing "horse race" predictions. The distinction between reporters and opin-ionists—particularly when it comes to campaign reporting—has been eroded almost completely, so that reporters now act as though they are commentators whose principal role it is, clairvoyant-like, to declare who will likely win and lose.

Beyond the deviation by journalists from the basic param-eters of fact reporting, it has become increasingly clear that the traveling press corps following the various candidates lives in an insular, segregated, profoundly out-of-touch bubble. The way they think about campaigns and elections could not be any further removed from how elections are perceived by the storied "average voter," on whose behalf the press corps ab-surdly fantasizes they speak.

For virtually all of 2007—with the first vote still months away—most ordinary voters paid little attention to the presi-dential campaign. As a result, the front-runner status of Clin-ton and Giuliani—like that of Joe Lieberman in 2004—was clearly a by-product of nothing more significant than superior name recognition, a fact which the politically obsessed report-ers were incapable of recognizing.

While the causes for this humiliating record of wrongness can be reasonably debated, its magnitude cannot be. Virtually every predictive pronouncement from the pundit class over the last year has been demonstrably and factually false. Yet the same pundits continue with the same behavior based on the same methods, never paying any price for their deeply flawed record. Being a pundit means never having to say you are sorry, or even admit that you are wrong. You just move seamlessly to the next story line, ignoring your past record of fundamental mistakes as though it never happened.

Journalists Should Publicly Disclose Any Payments Received

James Rainey

James Rainey is a reporter for the Los Angeles Times, *who focuses his investigations and analysis on the news media.*

Most reporters would love to make $75,000. In a year.

So it set my eyes to blinking when I read that *New York Times* columnist Thomas Friedman got paid that much for a single speech, sponsored last week [May 4, 2009] by the San Francisco Bay Area's clean air district.

I called the *Times,* several times in the last couple of days to ask Friedman a bunch of questions, like how it felt to be such a giant cheese, whether he would disclose who else paid him big bucks and whether he felt queasy taking so much money from a public agency that presumably could spend the money on other things.

Friedman didn't return my calls, and *New York Times* spokeswoman Catherine Mathis seemed pretty cool to my questions. I got the feeling, from her long silences, that she thought my questions were a little silly.

Then late Tuesday afternoon, Mathis called to say Friedman would return the $75,000. She said there had been "a misunderstanding."

The Risk of Conflicts of Interest

Times ethics guidelines allow staffers to take speaking fees only from "educational and other nonprofit groups for which lobbying and political activity are not a major focus." The Bay

James Rainey, "Thomas L. Friedman and the High Cost of Speaking: The New York Times Columnist Returns a $75,000 Speaking Fee," *Los Angeles Times*, May 13, 2009. Reproduced by permission.

Area Air Quality Management District, which coughed up Friedman's standard fee, hardly fits that bill.

So here's a tip of the reportorial green eye shade to Phil Matier and Andy Ross, the *San Francisco Chronicle* columnists who broke the story about the big payment. And here's a suggestion that the time has come for influential journalists like Friedman to disclose their substantial sources of outside income.

It seems only right that journalists—who spend a lot of time pressing public officials to disclose their income sources—start revealing potential conflicts of interest.

I don't have any reason to doubt Friedman's reputation as an earnest and dogged reporter. I read him enough to believe that his opinions, even ones I disagree with, flow from his heart and mind, not his wallet.

Still, it seems only right that journalists—who spend a lot of time pressing public officials to disclose their income sources—start revealing potential conflicts of interest. Some form of transparency will become even more important as a thousand new and unproven news sources bloom online.

Without the *Chronicle*'s dynamic reporting duo, the Bay Area air district would not be getting back its $75,000, money that could help cities expand bike paths or plant more trees.

That's proof enough for me that we can start the disclosure on these speaking engagements right here and now.

The Justification for Payment

When I talk at a high school or college, the hosts tend to provide a bottle of water. (I like it chilled, but sometimes I have to accept room temperature.) On rare occasions, I'll get comped a meal or a short road trip. Monday night, I spoke to Jim Burns' journalism students at Cal Poly Pomona. When it was over, the instructor handed me an envelope, containing a $25 Trader Joe's gift card.

Not that I expect to be paid like Friedman, who has a few things I don't, like three Pulitzer Prizes and a string of best-selling books, including *Hot, Flat, and Crowded: Why We Need a Green Revolution—and How It Can Renew America*.

I don't know, or really care, how Friedman spends his money. But it would be interesting and maybe revealing to see who else is willing to pay $75,000, which spokeswoman Mathis assured me is the "market rate."

The newspaper's ethics handbook requires journalists to file "an accounting" each January if they have earned more than $5,000 in speaking fees. Friedman passes that threshold just clearing his throat.

But Mathis told me the *New York Times* does not release the reports on speaking engagements it receives from its employees.

Before Friedman agreed to give back the money, the spokeswoman had been trying to help me understand why a $75,000 fee made good sense.

She noted that the columnist "flew across the country at their request" to make the appearance.

He conducted "a lengthy Q and A," she added, "so they were getting not only the presentation but a chance to talk with him and ask him questions."

Mathis noted that Friedman frequently waives his fee, as he planned to do in speaking this week to the Sierra Club.

And he makes his speeches and PowerPoint presentations available free of charge on his thomaslfriedman.com website.

She said, finally, that Friedman gives generously to charity.

The Issue of Disclosure

All good. But I'm still curious how Friedman decides who pays and who doesn't and how he would feel about matching my public disclosure.

Friedman's appearance in Oakland last week before about 500 bureaucrats had been in the works for more than a year.

His lecture agent arranged the appearance, Mathis told me. "He had been under the impression that it was a community group or nonprofit," she said. "When he found out it was not, he instructed his agent to return the fee and they have notified the organization."

It's hard to imagine that a practiced speaker like Friedman didn't know what sort of crowd he'd be addressing, especially since the whole point of the daylong "climate summit" was to inspire local government officials to promote sustainable development.

I'm guessing a more likely explanation is that Friedman and his agent hadn't focused on his paper's speaking guidelines recently and that the Oakland group didn't seem that much different to him from dozens of others he's addressed.

Public disclosure of large outside payments, say of $1,000 or more, would allow us to keep better tabs on what's driving the press.

Transparency About Political Views Is Preferable to Objectivity

Reed Richardson

Reed Richardson is managing editor for numerous national and regional print and online publications at Touchpoint Media.

At this year's [2009] White House Correspondents' Association dinner, the President introduced himself with a not-so-subtle poke at the Washington press corps: "I am Barack Obama. Most of you covered me. All of you voted for me." The joke elicited hearty laughter, but it also cut uncomfortably close to the bone at a time when many people regard the news media as politically biased, inaccurate and out of touch.

The Ethical Dilemma Journalists Face

This dour assessment of journalism's credibility—documented in the 2009 "State of the News Media" study by the Pew Research Center's Project for Excellence in Journalism—follows a nearly 20-year-long decline in the public's esteem for the press. Myriad reasons exist for this collapse, but a factor consistently overlooked involves the ethical dilemma—and a dispute among journalists—that lies at the heart of the President's joke: Where do journalists draw the line between objectively reporting on how well our democracy is functioning and personally participating in it?

Those who favor a more inclusive and engaged personal approach, melded with greater transparency, are still in the minority. "What this new ethic asks the reporter to do is to be honest in disclosing his or her point of view, his or her biases, his or her affiliations. Then in writing or producing his or her story, make it very clear that is the perspective from which it has come," explains Marc Cooper, a journalism professor at the University of Southern California.

This approach departs from the way most newsrooms operate today. Broad restrictions are reserved for conduct outside of the newsroom that is either unethical or illegal, while behavioral rules, such as those involving conflicts of interest for specialized beats, tend to be narrowly drawn.

Journalists' Free Speech

In handling editorial employees' right of free speech, nearly all major news organizations regard employment and political activity to be mutually exclusive. An extreme minority of journalists even swears off voting, yet no newsroom forbids reporters to vote. And in the era of Facebook and cell phone cameras, newsrooms are adopting a siege mentality as they further circumscribe what is acceptable behavior for their editorial employees. Pennsylvania State University journalism professor Gene Foreman, author of the 2009 book, *The Ethical Journalist*, supports such efforts: "We have to be as restrained as we can in getting involved in community life," he says. "You're kind of giving [the public] a stick to hit you with" by divulging political opinions in today's environment.

However, this notion of certifying journalists' neutrality by concealing political opinions seems shortsighted and hypocritical because it creates a distorted ethical landscape. A White House correspondent can cast a vote for Obama and socialize with administration officials without questions being raised about the independence of his reporting. Yet, if this reporter discloses his vote or drives a car with an Obama bumper sticker, his work is considered to be tainted.

In our digital times, news consumers increasingly seek news that is filtered through the partisan lens of cable TV and the blogosphere. Given this, these newsroom ethics rules appear anachronistic. "The way journalism is moving, I think people are much more interested in having a strong point of view in their news," says Eric Alterman, City University of New York journalism professor and media critic for *The Nation*. "A much better question is how does it affect the journalism, because you can be an incredible partisan and still be very fair."

Over time, the veneer of political impartiality devalues reporting and marginalizes the press's fundamental role in our democracy.

The Veneer of Impartiality

In June 2007, MSNBC.com investigative reporter Bill Dedman identified 143 working journalists—out of a total of roughly 100,000 nationwide—as having made campaign contributions during the previous four years. He made almost no effort, however, to find evidence linking these donations to biased coverage. Neither did the *Detroit Free Press*, which tried to ban all political donations by employees after two of its journalists' names surfaced in Dedman's story. An independent arbitrator struck down the newspaper's new ethics rule as unnecessarily broad and pointed out that despite the claim of harm to the paper's reputation, Executive Editor Caesar Andrews had conceded that the paper "did not possess or even look for evidence that [the donations] compromised the *Free Press*'s integrity."

Dedman told me that to focus solely on the fairness of journalistic output misses the point. "An umpire only has to cheer for the Red Sox during the game once to call his objectivity, his independence, into question," he contends, in drawing the analogy that many make of the press as serving the role of an impartial umpire. "It matters how he performs his job, yes, but it also matters that he appear not to take sides."

Over time, the veneer of political impartiality devalues reporting and marginalizes the press's fundamental role in our democracy. This stance leads to artificial "balanced" reporting and sound bite symmetry ("he said, she said") rather than what the reporter's role ought to be—seeking and conveying what is found to be true.

The Digital Push

Earlier this year, on his blog PressThink, Jay Rosen wrote "He Said, She Said Journalism: Lame Formula in the Land of the Active User." He observed that "Any good blogger, competing journalist or alert press critic can spot and publicize false balance and the lame acceptance of fact-free spin. Do users really want to be left helpless in sorting out who's faking it more? The he said, she said form says they do, but I say decline has set in."

News organizations ought to figure out ways to be more accepting of journalists' civic engagement and develop strategies to be transparent about it.

In Rosen's view, the Web's decentralized and horizontally connected ethos provides a healthy counterweight in giving citizen-generated reporting and partisan bloggers the same potential reach as established news organizations. As these unrestrained voices build audiences and gain legitimacy, newsrooms adapt; many now invite contributors from outside of the newsroom to post stories and images to their Web sites.

As this happens, tensions inevitably develop between the newsroom's strict ethics rules and the absence of similar standards for contributed content. This disparity was on display when Mayhill Fowler, *The Huffington Post*'s citizen reporter who broke the Obama "Bittergate" story last April [2008] got her scoop; as an Obama campaign donor, she was attending a private fundraising party closed to the press.

A demographic imperative will accelerate this change as those who've grown up with the Web's ethos of interactive opinion sharing, much of it political in nature, get involved in reporting news. Given this trend, news organizations ought to figure out ways to be more accepting of journalists' civic engagement and develop strategies to be transparent about it. Doing so would also help in repairing the press's tarnished reputation.

Reporters having a personal point of view should not prevent them from doing fair and accurate coverage.

Mechanisms and platforms exist, even if the willpower doesn't, to facilitate this ethical shift. On the Web, bylines link to short bios; in these, personal disclosure statements could appear to reveal a reporter's work history and educational background. If such a declaration is especially pertinent to a story, it could be prominently displayed in much the same way online corrections are now handled.

Protecting Free Speech Through Transparency

Embracing transparency is not an endorsement of an ethical free-for-all. "Common sense would rule out clearly unacceptable situations—a newspaper's political writer working on a campaign, say," wrote Will Bunch, a senior writer at the *Philadelphia Daily News*, in an *American Journalism Review* article on this topic. "But transparency would clear the way for reporters who wish to work in a battered women's shelter or maybe even that technology writer protesting the war in Iraq." In essence, newsrooms would treat editorial employees' political activity no differently than other public behavior, such as attending religious services or investing in real estate.

News organizations should realize that what sets their content apart is not their staff's eschewing of a campaign yard sign, but how they employ their skills to produce better reporting. Credibility is the press's authority; reporters having a personal point of view should not prevent them from doing fair and accurate coverage.

With an operating ethic of protecting reporters' free speech, the trade-off for journalists would be forgoing some measure of personal privacy. When they divulge information about their personal political engagement—other potential conflicts of interest, for example—the public will be able to assess the full dimensions of the news it receives.

Letting go of this fear of public awareness of reporters' political engagement and leanings won't be easy. This spring *The Washington Post* fired Dan Froomkin, whose White House Watch column, the paper's ombudsman wrote in 2005, made the *Post*'s political reporters uncomfortable because it was "highly opinionated and liberal." Froomkin argued that he was just doing what journalists should do. Now, as Washington bureau chief for *The Huffington Post* and at the Nieman Watchdog Web site, Froomkin has observed that "the sense that if you have a belief that you publicly espouse you can no longer be fair about reporting a subject is problematic. Reporters have beliefs, they have values—the key is for them not to let those beliefs unduly affect their reporting." There are principles, he says, that journalists should stand for—accountability, transparency, fair play, human rights—and "there's nothing wrong with journalists wearing those values on their sleeves."

There Is Nothing Wrong with Partisan Journalism

Jack Shafer

Jack Shafer is a columnist for Reuters news agency, covering the press and politics.

By suspending MSNBC *Countdown* anchor Keith Olbermann without pay for a grand total of two days, NBC News struck a suspiciously weak blow for its policy that requires employees to secure the permission of NBC News' president before they give to political campaigns.

News Shows That Are Partisan

If the network was hoping to telegraph that it doesn't think Olbermann's offense was much of an offense at all—the consensus view of his ideological soul-mates and even some of his ideological opponents—it succeeded hugely. According to *Politico*, Olbermann wouldn't have had to serve his suspension had he agreed to deliver an on-camera *mea culpa* [acknowledgment of fault].

But NBC still has some explaining to do. Has it established a new precedent—that, in the future, if any anchor or reporter gives $7,200 to candidates, as Olbermann did, he will suffer only two days in the dog house? Hell, next election cycle Olbermann should give $14,400 in exchange for four-day suspension, and other MSNBCers should take note of the network's punishment-per-incident equation and give accordingly.

The best way for the network to exit the morass it's created is to stop pretending that *Countdown* and *The Rachel*

Maddow Show are straight-news programs. Of course, there's plenty of straight news in both programs, just as straight news can be found in the *New Republic*, the *Nation*, the *Weekly Standard*, *Mother Jones*, the *National Review*, *Reason*, and other opinion magazines. But both anchors and both programs are so transparent about coming at the news from a liberal angle that it's the network's failing—not theirs—that the shows aren't billed as partisan takes on the news, as the magazines listed above are.

> *As long as the partisan journalist comes to verifiable conclusions, we shouldn't worry too much about the direction from which he came.*

The Fundamental Role of Partisan Journalism

At their best, American political magazines don't pretend to be bias-free. But they do subscribe to elementary standards of fairness and accuracy, which I've always thought were more important to good journalism than being independent of bias. A partisan journalist doesn't have to feign impartiality to do his work, which can sometimes be a plus. Like investigative reporters, partisan journalists hear frequencies outside the listening range of journalists who subscribe to the centrist ideology. On the great issues of the day, I'd rather read the best of what left-wing and right-wing journals had to say than I would the *Washington Post* or the *New York Times*. In fact, by publishing an op-ed section, a newspaper acknowledges the fundamental role partisan journalism plays in understanding politics and culture.

Take, for example, Maddow's respectful but prosecutorial grilling of then-candidate Rand Paul during his senatorial campaign. Maddow drew upon her partisanship to press the question of the Civil Rights Act on Paul. Or, I think I should say, a lack of worry on her part that she'll be busted for leveraging her own points of view in an interview with a politician gives Maddow real strength. Give me Rachel Maddow over Diane Sawyer any day.

Although not "objective" in the pedestrian sense of the word, these magazines generally attempt to verify the accuracy of their findings. As Bill Kovach and Tom Rosenstiel write in their 2001 book, *The Elements of Journalism*, traditionally, it was the journalistic *method* that was supposed to be objective, not the journalist. As long as the partisan journalist comes to verifiable conclusions, we shouldn't worry too much about the direction from which he came.

The Value of Opinion

Why can't MSNBC see the value in letting *Countdown* and *The Rachel Maddow Show* be what they want to be: well-reported, liberal opinion magazines that happen to air on television? Perhaps it's because MSNBC's strings are still controlled by NBC, which, as a holder of federal broadcast licenses for its TV and radio stations, had to uphold the fairness doctrine all those decades or face the revocation of its licenses. Even though the fairness doctrine is long dead, and stations no longer have to make sure that, if violet expresses its opinion on a show, its take must be balanced by a hearing of equal duration from the color orange. One of the causes of the Olbermann dust-up is the fact that the doctrine lives on in the institutional memories of the old networks like NBC, which controls MSNBC in a co-venture with Microsoft. Fox, which never really had to kowtow to the fairness doctrine, seems to be the least psychologically muzzled of any network, although I don't intend that as an endorsement of any Fox News Channel program.

I'm not advocating that every channel and every publication become an organ of opinion. But if it's OK for newspapers to run opinion columnists and opinion sections, then surely there's sufficient room in MSNBC's 24/7 stream of cable news for both. Instead of viewing Olbermann's partisanship as a liability, NBC should treat it as an asset. To paraphrase something Paul Starr once wrote to Michael Schudson, in the minds of many readers, the editorial pages of a newspaper vouchsafe the credibility of its news columns by saying here is opinion, and over here is fact. But making overt what is now covert—stating unequivocally that *Countdown* and *Maddow* are opinion magazines, and, hell yes, shredding that no-contribution-without-permission policy—the network could better brand these two shows and its other programs.

Likewise MSNBC's very nervous legacy parent, NBC News, which thinks itself tarnished by opinion on its cable child, could better distance itself from the Olbermann-Maddow Experience. So, yes, free Keith, free Rachel, and by all means, free MSNBC.

Questioning
Journalistic Objectivity

Courtney Martin

Courtney Martin is the author of Do It Anyway: The New Generation of Activists *and* Project Rebirth: Survival and the Strength of the Human Spirit from 9/11 Survivors.

Journalism, as we've known it, has been mourned deeply over the last few years. The Internet has changed everything. "Citizen journalism," a phrase that still inspires dirty looks at most journalism conferences, has blurred the lines between objectivity and subjectivity, paid and unpaid labor, news and opinion. It gives veteran journalists agita to imagine totally untrained people messing around in their exclusive, albeit hardscrabble, club.

With all this reshaping and shifting of our industry, all this talk about changing financial models and publishing structures, now is an opportune time to question one of the field's most defended values: objectivity.

This issue has been particularly present for me as I'm on the final stages of writing a book—a collection of profiles of ten people under 35 who are doing interesting social justice work. It's been necessarily intimate; these are 8,000 word, very in-depth, largely psychological profiles. They require a level of openness, on the part of the subject, and a level of listening, on the part of the journalist, that surpasses any of the shorter, less personal genres. In my interviews for this book, I've discussed a range of sensitive and difficult topics: physical abuse, immigration, class, gender identity, rape, divorce, death, race, and birth. I've sat in my subjects' offices, favorite restaurants, and classrooms, taken walks with them through their childhood neighborhoods, cried over their suffering, rejoiced with them over their victories.

After asking my subjects to be so trusting, so transparent, and so generous with their time, I feel compelled to make them feel safe in the experience of being written about—an inherently objectifying and frightening prospect. I made clear that I wasn't planning on writing glowing press releases about them, instead aiming to be honoring and honest, empathic and compassionately critical.

We each come to our lives and the lives of others with a lens worn and weathered over years of learning, experiences, and social conditioning.

And I told them that I would show them drafts and give them a chance to give me feedback and correct inaccuracies before the pieces become public.

Here's where I can almost hear the journalism professors scream, "Stop the presses!" The traditional journalistic approach is to conduct your interviews and experience a connection with your subjects, then sit in a room and write about it, removing them from the process—except perhaps for some cut-and-dried fact checking (such as "confirm the date of your birth, your first wife's name, and the spelling of your alma mater"). If I was following this convention, I would transcribe, write, revise with my editor's guidance, and publish. End of story.

The argument for sticking with the traditional method is fairly straight-forward—people will want to meddle with "the real story." Journalists have to create bonds, and then break them, in honor of the larger goal: Truth (with a capital "T"). Besides, no one ever thinks they've said anything the way they've actually said it—even when you play the tape back for them. Giving them a chance to comment prepublication is a fool's errand.

There is certainly wisdom in this, but it denies the dynamic of human perception. We each come to our lives and the lives of others with a lens worn and weathered over years of learning, experiences, and social conditioning. We don't see others—even in seemingly banal situations—through a pristine, ahistorical point of view; we see them through a unique assemblage of all the prior references we have, all of our prejudices—conscious and unconscious, all of our own fears and passions. To deny that is to deny human nature.

The goal contemporary journalists should strive toward—at least in long, reflective form—is not objectivity.

And beyond that, there's a rarely talked about but very powerful reason that journalists hide behind this convention. It's not just that we want to uphold Truth. It's incredibly frightening to think that you're going to have to be accountable to real people in the writing process. It's much easier to pretend that your master is Fact (with a capital "F") and call it a day. Facts don't speak back—unless you get them egregiously wrong and then people speak back for them. Even then, you might be seen as careless, but usually not insensitive. Your effectiveness and credibility, not your humanity, is at stake.

Opening yourself up to feedback from your subjects is frightening, yes, but it's still not as scary as being written about. Becoming the subject of a journalistic piece is objectifying. Even when I write about myself, I cringe at being exposed. It's like having just one snapshot of yourself projected on a giant billboard. It's you, indeed, but it's only one version of you. So of course I understand how complex, strange, and sometimes offensive it can be for others to be shaped into a caricature of my own making.

That's why I'm deeply committed to this collaborative process of talking and listening, writing and responding, editing and reflecting *with* my subjects. That's the least I owe them, and rather than discouraging a poignant or honest portrait, I think it often enhances my work. The courage it takes to write about people as I really see them, flaws and all, is related to the courage it takes for them to expose themselves, and then engage in the process of commenting on my portrayal. This congruency seems to support a certain sort of magic on the page—a process of mutual pursuit of a truth, rather than a one-sided, hubristic claim on the Truth.

The goal contemporary journalists should strive toward—at least in long, reflective form—is not objectivity. The goal should be, as Pulitzer Prize-winning journalist Jack Fuller put it in *Shop Talk & War Stories*, "work of genuine intellectual integrity," and I would add emotional accountability. It might be messier, but it's ultimately more transformative.

Objectivity Should Be Secondary to Morality

Adam Weinstein

Adam Weinstein is a national security reporter for Mother Jones, *specializing in civil-military relations, budgeting, and nuclear policy.*

So, apparently Bill Nye the Science Guy was giving this speech to a bunch of Southern California [USC] students Tuesday [November 16, 2010] when he tripped over an extension cord, knocked his head, spoke some gibberish, and fainted onstage. And the crowd just sat there, with nary a good Samaritan among them, live tweeting the series of unfortunate events till Bill came around of his own accord. Twitty Twitterers? You bet. A sad commentary on the youngs and their gawker culture? Perhaps.

A Defense of Journalistic Objectivity

But journalist David Axe has a different takeaway from the audience's unresponsiveness. A young war correspondent for the likes of *Wired* and the *Washington Times*, Axe writes on his group blog *War Is Boring* that "this 'passivity' could also be something else: journalistic 'objectivity.'" Then he gets weirdly personal:

> Two years ago, I took the time to videotape a gunshot man dying on a street during a battle in Abeche, Chad. I did not try to help the man as he lay at my feet. I fled only when someone opened fire in my direction. . . .

Adam Weinstein, "Are Good Journalists 'All Bad People?,'" *Mother Jones*, November 17, 2010. www.motherjones.com © 2010, Foundation for National Progress. All rights reserved. Reproduced by permission.

Asked about the incident a year later, I said it never occurred to me to help the man. It was my job to document the battle and its victims. If forced to choose between trying to save the life of someone I did not know, or recording his slow death so that I might highlight its tragedy, I suppose I will usually choose the latter. I am not a medic. I am not a decent person. I am a journalist.

And so are the USC students, in a sense. The more we equip ourselves with the technology to document our own lives and events around us, the more we might see merely observing as a role—and an important one. In that sense, it's hypocritical for any journalist to criticize the students for watching rather than acting. For if they are a good journalist, they would have done the very same thing.

A False Dichotomy

I'm pretty big into the social media, so for now I'll accept Axe's glib assertions that every roomful of students with smartphones is a roomful of journalists, and journalism is "merely observing." The bigger problem is Axe's cynical description of the news reporter as an amoralist. You can be a good person who cares about other human beings, or you can be a good journalist. You can try to save a life, or you can be "objective." But you can't be both.

> *There's nothing potentially more dangerous in journalism than using "objectivity" as a pretense to practice amorality.*

It's a false dichotomy, of course. Journalistic objectivity is what we make of it. And if we make it completely devoid of a moral core, then we fail epically *both* as journalists and human beings. Believe it or not, you *can* actually do a good deed in the middle of a reporting job and still tell the story.

But in the Chad shooting, Axe did neither. Here's his *Washington Times* writeup.

... a reporter witnessed men dressed in military fatigues shooting at each other throughout downtown Abeche. One young man dressed in a mix of civilian and military clothes bled and died while soldiers and fleeing civilians stepped over him.

This excerpt is hardly "objective": Axe gets an emotional reaction out of the reader by depicting "soldiers and fleeing civilians" stepping over the dying man ... while neglecting to mention that he, too, paced around the poor Chadian. Strangely, though, in the video he filmed of the incident, Axe comes off as the star: He titled it "Getting Shot At." (The video also shows that Axe made a tragically poor judgment, shining a light on the dying man in the middle of a pitch-black night—which brought a predictable hail of gunfire down on both him and the bleeding victim.)

The Power of Journalism

The takeaway: There's nothing potentially more dangerous in journalism than using "objectivity" as a pretense to practice amorality. News reporting doesn't exist in a vacuum; it isn't good in itself. It's supposed to be good *for something*: Selling papers, educating citizens, exposing injustices or inhumanities, whatever. There's always some higher value at play when a journalist is at work.

I get what Axe is *trying* to say. One of the biggest problems with paid journalists—commenters point it out *a lot*—is our tendency to overinflate our moral worth. We want to do work that Matters, that Makes a Difference in the World. It's a good aspiration. *Mother Jones* exists because of it. But like all virtues, this one becomes a vice in megadoses. We all know that guy, the self-important reporter who thinks every hackneyed clause he spills into a Word file has the salvational properties of John 3:16. The one who claims no pretense to objectivity, which is good, since he's totally subjective. (You're reading one now.) Yeah, that's dangerous. But not as dangerous as grabbing a camera or notepad to report the news while leaving your moral scruples at home.

Now, Axe and his *War Is Boring* colleagues are very talented, and they all evidently believe in the power of journalism to transform society: They identify themselves on the site as "citizen journalists" with an interest in "peacekeeping over war-making." Before his cynicism gets much worse, Axe should consider that mission statement anew. After all, it's the "citizen" that comes first, not the "journalist."

CHAPTER 4

How Have New Technologies Affected Media Ethics?

Overview: Technologies That Have Changed Journalism

10,000 Words: Where Journalism and Technology Meet

10,000 Words: Where Journalism and Technology Meet is a blog published by mediabistro.com, which is a property of Web-MediaBrands, a leading internet company for creative and media professionals.

In the last few decades, the journalism industry has been rocked by an explosion of technology that has changed how news is gathered, reported, distributed, and shared. The following are the key technologies that have aided in the transformation of news:

The Digital Audio Recorder

Before digital audio recorders, there was the reel-to-reel machine, a clunky device that required the operator to physically splice pieces of tape together to form an audio story. Fast forward a few years later and the digital audio recorders have made the machine obsolete and changed audio recording forever.

Digital audio recorders allow journalists to go wherever they wish with what amounts to a tiny recording studio in their pocket. Digital recorders allow for quick, off-the-cuff recording of a news subject or interview and drastically cut down the time necessary to edit and broadcast the recording. In addition, digital recorders also allow the user to connect to a computer and within minutes publish the audio to the web, a concept that decades ago was unimaginable.

The Rise of Social Networks

Before there was MySpace, Facebook, or Twitter, there was Friendster, the online community that popularized the concept of the social network. Even though the site has waned in popularity, it opened the door for hundreds of thousands of social networks. The number of social network users around the world totals in the billions, with Facebook alone comprising more than 500 million members.

For journalists, social networks enable reporters and newsrooms to interact directly with the people and the communities they cover. A large percentage of any online news operation's web traffic comes from social networks as users recommend and share individual stories, rather than individual publications, with each other. Social networks have also replaced online news sites as destinations for news and allow audiences to shape and filter the news that reaches them.

Reporters can now write, record or edit video or audio, or broadcast live directly from a laptop computers and from anywhere around the world.

Mobile Devices and Other Tools

The iPhone, a device not without its flaws, is largely responsible for introducing the concept of applications to the public, eventually shaping mobile devices into mobile news readers. More than 24 percent of Americans now use apps regularly, more than half of which are news-related, according to a 2010 Pew study. The iPhone has accustomed audiences to paying for digital and mobile content and of course paved the way for a new generation of e-readers used for news consumption.

When Google Maps, and more importantly its API [application programming interface], first hit newsrooms, the technology was often used on a smaller scale to post small embeddable maps that accompanied stories. As newsrooms matured, Google Maps was used to create complex, location-based databases that not only categorized, but also visualized information. Google Maps in essence made data-driven journalism—both the production and consumption—accessible to everyone and transformed what would otherwise be unsightly charts and graphs into more user-friendly ways of displaying information. Maps, to this day, remain an important component of multimedia storytelling.

Who knew that a site that hosted videos of dancing cats and college pranks would become an online destination where an average of two billion videos are viewed daily and hundreds of thousands of videos are uploaded every day. YouTube conditioned audiences to watch online video and more of it and opened the door for both broadcast and non-broadcast newsrooms to publish and share video content online. YouTube not only empowered average citizens to upload and share their videos with a worldwide audience, it also transformed news video from siloed broadcasts to content that is freely shared and embedded on the web.

Laptops and Wireless Internet

Attend any press conference, news event, or media gathering and you're likely to see a crowd of reporters with laptops in hand documenting what is happening in front of them. The typewriter and the desktop computer both revolutionized modern journalism, but it is the laptop computer that freed reporters from the confines of the newsroom. As laptops become more powerful and inexpensive, they now often serve as a mobile multimedia production lab. Reporters can now write, record or edit video or audio, or broadcast live directly from a laptop computers and from anywhere around the world.

A laptop wouldn't be as revolutionary a tool for journalists if it weren't for wireless internet. Wi-fi puts the library of information contained on the web at a reporter's fingertips. Wireless internet also allows journalists to report from the field and file stories without having to physically return to the newsroom. As a Pew study notes, people are actually consuming more news than they used to and much of it is accessed online. There are many factors as to why this is, but it is likely due in large part to the pervasiveness of wireless internet and the many opportunities for news consumption the technology affords.

All of the aforementioned technologies were developed or rose in popularity within the last few decades. Who knows what new technology will emerge that will also change the face of journalism?

Digital Media Has Caused an Erosion of Ethical Standards

Bob Steele

Bob Steele is the Nelson Poynter Scholar for Journalism Values at The Poynter Institute, in St. Petersburg, Florida.

"Some of us feel like page-view whores, and it's got to stop."

With those words, a newspaper editor who e-mailed me in the summer of 2007 said what many of his colleagues have come to believe. It was an expression—an admission, really—of what many editors acknowledge has happened in the full-throttle race on the digital speedway fueled by a feverish fight for financial survival.

An Increase in Ethical Dilemmas

In my nearly two decades on the faculty of The Poynter Institute, I have fielded thousands of ethical queries from editors, reporters, producers, photojournalists and a good handful of news corporation executives. I'm generally heartened by the sincerity of the journalists in wanting to do the right thing ethically, and I cheer the remarkable reporting that is still produced in the face of considerable obstacles. Nevertheless, I'm very worried about the significant erosion of ethical standards across our profession and the resulting corrosion of the quality of the journalism. The blogs, Tweets, social networking, citizen-submitted content, and multimedia storytelling that are the tools and techniques of the digital era offer great promise. They also, when misused, present considerable peril.

Situations that editors confront in this digital-era maelstrom reflect the vexing ethical challenges and the diminished quality control standards at a time when they are most needed. Several examples I've been involved with exemplify the importance of renewing a commitment to time-honored ethical values that will build and protect the integrity of the journalism as it morphs into new forms of reporting, storytelling and delivery.

The editor who penned the "whores" self-description had asked me for input on what he termed "a not-very-good story this morning re: hate crimes." That news story included information from a community blog, information that ostensibly described what the alleged victim of the hate crime had done to prompt an attack. The editor wanted to know my view about whether putting the news story on the site of a traditional newspaper—with this additional information in it—gives the blog content false credibility.

It's bad when time-honored journalistic values of accuracy and fairness are eroded in the quest to draw eyeballs to the Web-generated stories.

The Challenges in Reporting on Blogs

I read the story and absorbed many of the reader comments attached to the Web site's version of that story. My response to the editor addressed both the blogs-as-news-content issue and the vile tone and tenor of certain reader posts to the story. Here's what I wrote in an e-mail to the editor:

I fear that many papers/reporters/editors are so caught up in the "search for eyeballs and page views" that the default position is often "let's put that blog stuff" in our story because "it's out there and folks are talking about it." We'll then "balance" the piece with concerns expressed by others connected to the story who have a different view than the bloggers.

Too often we give unjustified credibility to bloggers who are, at best, practicing amateur journalism or simplistic punditry. And news organizations provide that false credibility by equating the bloggers' observations and views with the rigor of news reporting. My point is similar to what Bill Kovach and Tom Rosenstiel emphasize in *The Elements of Journalism: What Newspeople Should Know and the Public Should Expect*, when they contrast assertion with verification. The latter is a purposeful process that seeks and reports the truth as best as possible. The former merely declares something based on little or no reliable fact-finding and thin, if any, confirmation.

I also told the editor it's bad when time-honored journalistic values of accuracy and fairness are eroded in the quest to draw eyeballs to the Web-generated stories. And it's a bad thing when there are serious negative consequences to those who are caught up in news stories, whether it's a dead man who can't defend himself to the blogger's pejorative descriptions of him or a victim's family members who are re-victimized by the hate, scorn, mocking and ridicule that are part of the comments posted to a news story.

Some readers' comments posted to the hate crime story—presumably ones that violated the paper's posting standards—had been excised. But other posts remaining I believed clearly pushed beyond the paper's standards against offensive name-calling and racist and bigoted commentary.

The editor, who I believe cares deeply about both the quality of the journalism and the ethics of the profession, responded with the *mea culpa* [acknowledgment of fault] I cited above. While I know this editor does not want to be a "page-view whore," I also recognize that he and his peers are under immense pressure to save the franchise. That means big-time risk taking and, in this era of staff cutbacks, it also means decreased editorial oversight and diminished checks and balances. Quality control suffers and quality deteriorates.

The Challenge of Social Networking

This ethical pressure cooker is reflected, too, in the thoughts of a managing editor at a metro paper who called me in October 2008. This editor wanted input on how to handle the increasing use of social networking by the paper's news staffers. Indeed, that paper's editors had advocated more blogging and Twittering, including on the personal sites of the newspaper's journalists. The goal: to spur reader interest and potentially more online user connection. The alarm bells started ringing when the managing editor noticed that one staffer's Tweets included what the editor termed "snarky" comments about a political candidate, comments laced with both opinion and obscenities.

Some of the ethics crashes on the digital media highway have generated national attention.

Just as that editor recognized that loose oversight had created an ethics problem that necessitated reaffirming some core values, the editor of *The* (Cleveland) *Plain Dealer* knew there was a serious problem when her paper's Web site prematurely reported the death of an Ohio congresswoman. "The speed of information is causing us to make mistakes," Susan Goldberg told a Kent State University forum on online ethics in September 2008.

Goldberg said that error would never have been made in the print version of the story because the facts would have been confirmed. "I don't want us to be wrong. I don't want our newspaper to be wrong," she said. "Mistakes can be damaging to our credibility. We're on a big stage, and we have a loud voice." She also declared that an "experiment is not working" when their political blogger became actively involved in the campaign of a local congressman.

Other editors have called me to seek guidance when they discovered that staff journalists were touting politicians or political causes on their personal Facebook pages. In most cases, the editors had not proactively addressed these conflict of interest issues until after a problem surfaced. Then it was more challenging to respond and in some cases to negotiate new ethics policy language with the guild representing the paper's journalists.

The Dangers of Fast Reporting

Some of the ethics crashes on the digital media highway have generated national attention. The accuracy and fairness concerns can be multiplied by the increasing use of so-called citizen journalists to provide reports that are then disseminated—often without verification—by traditional news organizations. Take the example of an October 2008 story that speaks loudly to the dangers of fast and furious reporting complicated by the minimal sourcing of the information.

For a period of time, CNN had a report on its iReport site (a user-submitted site where the content comes from the community) that claimed Apple CEO [chief executive officer] Steve Jobs had suffered a major heart attack. The story was not true, but Apple's stock took a quick dive with company shares off by more than 10 percent before the CNN iReport story on Jobs was debunked and removed from the site.

While many editors tout their ability to quickly take down factually wrong information or other egregious content, the damage done can be significant.

The Use of New Tools

Sometimes it's the tools journalists are using or just poor techniques with the tools that are ethically problematic. The *Rocky Mountain News* in Denver was roundly criticized for insensitivity in the funeral coverage of a three-year-old boy. A *Rocky* reporter used Twitter, a microblogging tool, to live-blog details from the graveside to the paper's Web site.

In the wake of significant backlash, *Rocky Mountain News* Editor John Temple wrote to readers that he accepted responsibility for any failing in the Twitter technique used in that situation, though he felt there was justifiable news value in the event that warranted this kind of unique coverage. "We must learn to use the new tools at our disposal," Temple wrote in his newspaper and on its Web site. "Yes, there are going to be times we make mistakes, just as we do in our newspaper. But that doesn't mean we shouldn't try something. It means we need to learn to do it well. That is our mission."

Now is the time to reaffirm essential core values that underpin journalism ethics and journalistic excellence.

The Need to Reaffirm Core Values

Which takes us full circle back to the importance of quality control as editors and other journalists search for that "true north" point on the moral compass. In recent years, many editors across the land learned hard lessons about the necessity of vigorous oversight on staff work. High-profile plagiarism and fabrication cases at papers the likes of *The New York Times, USA Today, The Boston Globe, The Seattle Times*, and *The Sacramento Bee* set off alarms. And in many of those cases the sinners were not the wet-behind-the-ears, youthful journalists but long-in-the-tooth veterans who succumbed to sin.

Editors recognized they needed better systems of quality control to deter liars and sinners. They needed clear, strong standards for attribution and a checks and balances process that prosecuted the work of all reporters and columnists, even those who had earned trust over the years. Those oversight lessons can and should be applied in the digital arena where writers can be tempted to cut corners on attribution as they rapidly source stories across the Internet.

Journalists—from reporters to multimedia producers to editors—are under great pressure to do more with less. The intense financial forces, the thinner staffs, and the risk-taking culture create a mixture where heightened quality control measures are all the more essential. Now is the time to reaffirm essential core values that underpin journalism ethics and journalistic excellence. Accuracy, fairness and honesty are as important now as they have ever been.

We must not let journalism turn horrific. Nor can we allow ourselves to become page-view whores.

The Rise in Nontraditional Reporting Requires a New Definition of Journalism

Ann Cooper

Ann Cooper is the CBS Professor of Professional Practice in International Journalism at Columbia University Graduate School of Journalism, in New York City.

In the late 1990s, the staff at the Committee to Protect Journalists [CPJ] in New York took note of an exciting new trend in China. With traditional Chinese media under tight state censorship, people with something critical to say about their government had seized on the Internet as a new platform to publish their views. Their actions were not unlike the samizdat dissidents of the Soviet era or the poster-makers of Beijing University during the 1989 student uprising. But now, with the Internet, Chinese writers had the potential to reach a global audience.

The Role of the Nontraditional Journalist

In 1999, China arrested six people on charges of using the Internet to spread "anti-government" or "subversive" messages. I was the executive director of CPJ at the time, and we had to decide whether to take up their cases. None was a journalist in any traditional sense; reporting wasn't their daily job and they didn't write for established news organizations. But they were, we reasoned, acting journalistically. They disseminated news, information, and opinion. We took up the cases.

In the years since, CPJ has defended writers in Cuba, Iran, Malaysia, and elsewhere—some traditional journalists, some not—who used the Internet to get around official censorship. In CPJ's view, these were entrepreneurial spirits using technology to battle enemies of press freedom. The many American journalists who supported CPJ's global work readily agreed.

Freedom of the press now belongs not just to those who own printing presses, but also to those who use cell phones, video cameras, blogging software, and other technology.

Media Ethics

Yet what U.S. journalists recognized as a press-freedom breakthrough in China and Cuba looked different here at home. Here, the Internet wasn't a thrilling way to dodge government censors. It was a platform for new competitors who seemed to take particular glee in lambasting the gatekeepers of mainstream media. In the view of some online writers, American journalism was calcified, too self-important to correct its errors or own up to its biases, too pompous to talk *with* its audience, rather than *at* it. The newcomers soon surrounded the tent of traditional journalism, demanding fundamental, maybe revolutionary, change. Many inside the tent huffed that the online competitors were not "real" journalists. They were acerbic ego-trippers, publishers of opinion and unconfirmed gossip with no professional standards. They stole the hard work of mainstream reporters and rarely picked up a telephone to do their own research. Some said bloggers threatened the established order of American journalism, and maybe even American democracy.

The Expansion of Journalism

And so it went for a few years, bloggers versus journalists; a fight over much more than semantics, a fight to see whether the big tent of American journalism would become a bigger tent to accommodate the newcomers and their new ideas. Who belongs in that tent, and who gets to decide who's in it? Put another way: Who is a journalist? It's a tantalizing question, but it's hardly worth asking anymore. *We're All Journalists Now* declared Washington lawyer Scott Gant's 2007 book, subtitled *The Transformation of the Press and Reshaping of the Law in the Internet Age*. A less sexy but perhaps more accurate title might have been, *We Can All Be Journalists, If and When We Choose to Be*. But Gant's basic point is sound: freedom of the press now belongs not just to those who own printing presses, but also to those who use cell phones, video cameras, blogging software, and other technology to deliver news and views to the world—just like those early Internet writers in China.

The expansion of the tent brings questions and challenges, of course—for institutions (who gets press passes?), for the law (how do you draft a shield bill if anyone can be a journalist?), and for journalists themselves (what are the standards of my profession?). Here's a field report—snapshots, really—on how we're all adapting to a fluid situation.

A Credentialing Dilemma

Soon after former radio and wire-service journalist Jim Van Dongen became a spokesman for the New Hampshire Department of Safety in 2003, he found himself confronted with press-pass applications from unpaid Internet bloggers and community-radio talk-show hosts. His first reaction: they're not "legitimate" journalists. His second reaction: we need a definition of who is.

It was Van Dongen's third reaction that was surprising. After trying out different criteria—journalists write for pay; they do original reporting, not just opinion writing—Van Dongen concluded that none of the criteria worked. In today's digital world, he says, "essentially, anybody who says he's a journalist is one." So this past January [2008], Van Dongen's office announced that it would no longer issue press passes. "Either we must issue such ID to virtually anyone who asks for it or be placed in the position of deciding who is or is not a legitimate journalist. That is not an appropriate role for a state agency," the department said in a January 15 news advisory. Though stunning in its symbolism, the New Hampshire decision didn't have much practical effect; Safety Department press passes were rarely needed, except for access to the state legislature floor.

Barriers will continue to erode, at least for bloggers who have credibility and an audience.

Nor have other institutions rushed to copy Van Dongen's response to the credentialing dilemma. In institutional worlds such as government, politics, and business, many in charge of press operations still cast a wary eye at requests from outside mainstream media. It's not that they're inundated with applicants; many institutions say blogger requests are still something of a novelty. But they're not at all sure what to do with someone who doesn't look like a traditional journalist. Last January [2008], for example, the retail chain Target e-mailed blogger Amy Jussel to say it wouldn't answer her questions about its ad campaigns because "Target does not participate with non-traditional media outlets." Meanwhile, the New York Civil Liberties Union went to court in February to force the release of all recent New York Police Department [NYPD] decisions on press-pass requests; the action is aimed at determining whether, as some independent online writers claim, the NYPD denies cards to applicants who don't work in the journalistic mainstream.

An Increase in Access

But institutional barriers are definitely crumbling. Bloggers were admitted to the 2004 and 2008 political party conventions. They had reserved seating in a spillover room at the

January 2007 trial of former White House aide Scooter Libby. Doors have cracked open at the United Nations, the White House, and the congressional press galleries, which have all accredited online-only journalists. So have legislatures in California, Tennessee, and Georgia, according to Michelle Blackston, a spokeswoman for the National Conference of State Legislatures. Blackston's group counsels an inclusive press policy—urging lawmakers to leak good stories to bloggers, and to start their own blogs. "We feel strongly it's a new way for lawmakers to connect with their constituents," she says.

That is precisely why barriers will continue to erode, at least for bloggers who have credibility and an audience. If their message reaches people newsmakers want to reach, their requests for press credentials and other access will be taken as seriously as those from mainstream media.

The Legal Risks

Few issues have united mainstream media like their effort to pass a federal shield law, which would give journalists some immunity from having to reveal confidential sources to federal courts. But the number one legal issue for traditional media—which is not expected to win final congressional approval this year [2008]—hasn't stirred a lot of passion in the blogosphere, where writers attract readers with their opinionated take on events much more than with original reporting. In fact, blog writers face a very different set of legal risks from those addressed in the shield law. Bloggers, says Robert Cox, an online writer and president of the Media Bloggers Association, "are going to be intentionally provocative. They rely on hyperbole, sometimes." Cox says that several hundred lawsuits have been filed against bloggers, most charging defamation, copyright violation, or invasion of privacy.

Mainstream journalists can avoid such charges by turning to editors or in-house lawyers for advice; company insurance also provides protection if they're sued. In the blogosphere, editors are few and far between, insurance is costly, and legal help is usually limited to consulting a nonprofit resource—like Cox's group, or the Citizen Media Law Project at Harvard University. "There are some simple things bloggers can do" without compromising their passionate voices, says Cox, "but they don't know to do them." Something as basic, for example, as using the disclaimer "alleged" when writing about a person accused but not convicted of a crime. "The more professional you are, the better your standards, the more defensible your position," says Cox.

> These days it's more the act of journalism that gets you entry into the tent, not whether you're doing it every day, or doing it for pay.

But that advice, like the online law course Cox's group plans to offer to help bloggers get insurance, isn't always well received in the fiercely independent blogosphere. "There's an extreme sensitivity to anyone trying to tell some other blogger what to do," Cox acknowledges.

The Old and New Journalists

"Bloggers vs. journalists is over," declared a January 2005 post by Jay Rosen, a journalism professor at New York University who writes prolifically about the new world of journalism at his site PressThink. "The question now isn't whether blogs can be journalism. They can be, sometimes. It isn't whether bloggers 'are' journalists. They apparently are, sometimes. We have to ask different questions now because events have moved the story forward."

When Rosen wrote that almost four years ago, events hadn't moved nearly far enough to convince many mainstream journalists that the debate was over. But in 2008, with old media in a financial crisis that seems to deepen by the week, resistance is evaporating. Traditional reporters and online writers are increasingly converging under one shared journalistic tent, where each side is free to borrow from the other. Thus, mainstream reporters still write news and analysis that strive for impartiality, but increasingly they also blog (at midsummer, nytimes.com had sixty-one news and opinion blogs; there were eighty-one at washingtonpost.com). Bloggers still aggregate and riff off the news reported in mainstream media, but a few are beginning to draw readers with original reporting.

These days it's more the *act* of journalism that gets you entry into the tent, not whether you're doing it every day, or doing it for pay. There are still distinctions, though. "Old" journalists are called professional, traditional, mainstream, or institutional; "new" ones are amateur, nontraditional, nonprofessional, or citizen journalists. PressThink's Rosen promotes "pro-am" experiments, in which unpaid citizen writers like Mayhill Fowler (who broke the [Barack] Obama "bittergate" story for Huffington Post) work with professional editors like Marc Cooper (a journalism professor and former contributing editor at *The Nation*) to cover the news in different ways.

Does this mean we're one big happy family in the big new tent? Far from it. In an interview, Rosen said many bloggers still fume that they have second-class status; even when they break news, "there's still a sense that a story hasn't really arrived until it's picked up by the mainstream media." And while some traditionalists may be enjoying the breezier writing style that blogging allows, they wonder what it's doing to journalism's hallowed standards.

A Call for Regulation

Last December [2007], former NBC correspondent David Hazinski unloaded his traditional-journalist concerns on *The Atlanta Journal-Constitution*'s op-ed page. Hazinski, a journalism professor at the University of Georgia, railed against television's increasing reliance on a new form of citizen journalism—video shot by nonprofessionals, like CNN's *iReports*.

Calling a citizen iReporter a journalist, said Hazinski, "is like saying someone who carries a scalpel is a 'citizen surgeon' or someone who can read a law book is a 'citizen lawyer.'" What distinguishes a journalist from the average citizen who records news on his or her cell phone, said Hazinski, are education, skill, and standards. "Information without journalistic standards is called gossip," he concluded.

The blogosphere dumped a blizzard of "absolute hatred" on Hazinski, "I had death threats;" he says. Most were rejecting his suggestion that a lack of standards for citizen journalism "opens up information flow to the strong probability of fraud and abuse. The news industry should find some way to monitor and regulate this new trend." The more irate responders reminded Hazinski that mainstream media's record on fraudulent reporting was far from unblemished, and that his vague call to "monitor and regulate" wasn't likely to be embraced even by mainstream journalists, in a country where the media tend to equate "regulation" of their industry with censorship.

It may be possible to build a new journalism, combining, for example, the best of traditional shoe-leather reporting with exciting new citizen-journalist teams.

Underneath Hazinski's provocative phrasing is an important point, though: let's not cast aside good journalism's goals and values simply because there are new ways to report and present the news. At the same time, let's do see if some of the rules need rethinking and adjustment to fit the new realities. That Mayhill Fowler article on Obama's "bitter" remarks sparked one fierce, and useful, ethical debate. Fowler recorded Obama at a fundraiser that she was able to attend only because she had contributed to his campaign, a move that violates the ethics codes of major U.S. news organizations. Yet even as Fowler's newsgathering strategies were being debated, her scoop—followed and amplified by the mainstream press— became an important new narrative in the election. No one denied that what she reported was important. "But if the old rules are fading away," wrote Michael Tomasky, who edits *Guardian America*, "there have to be a few new ones to take their place. There can't just be anarchy."

Building a New Journalism

Draft ethics codes have circulated in the blogosphere, and the ideas in drafts posted at CyberJournalist.net and on the sites of bloggers such as Rebecca Blood and Tim O'Reilly would be familiar to those who've worked in major media newsrooms. It would be wrong, though, to assume that the blogosphere is likely to organize itself into mainstream-style professional groups with industry-wide standards (for that matter, mainstream media don't follow one set of standards). "The blogosphere has no organization, None. It's chaotic. That's what makes it vibrant," said Rosen.

When I asked Eric Umansky, a senior writer at the investigative journalism project ProPublica (and a cjr contributing editor) and a veteran of both old and new media, how standards of online journalism will be enforced, his answer was one that's repeated often in cyberspace: "It's going to be regulated essentially by the marketplace." That means a blog, just like a newspaper, has to build credibility; people will stop reading if it's "unreliable and unlikely to tell me anything new," he said. The marketplace solution is not particularly reassuring to many traditional journalism gatekeepers. They don't want mandatory standards, but as they open up their own thinking about the online world, they do want the blogosphere to recognize that journalism won't survive on any platform without a common belief in some principles—among them, a commitment to accuracy and to avoiding (or clearly revealing) conflicts of interest. In one of his most recent ruminations on the transitional world of journalism, Rosen described the gatekeepers as a "tribe" now migrating from the failing business model of old journalism to a new digital platform. The migration, he said, offers the opportunity to build a hybrid model with online journalists.

Rosen's hybrid notion shifts the focus from defining "who is a journalist" to "what is journalism." That's a necessary shift, and once it's made, it may be possible to build a new journalism, combining, for example, the best of traditional shoe-leather reporting with exciting new citizen-journalist teams. But a hybrid would require true collaboration between old and new practitioners who are serious about sustaining journalism and its public-service mission. Old media will have to let go of some attitudes and assumptions that are no longer relevant, and new media will need to recognize standards that can infuse credibility and trust into this new journalism. Working together will require everyone in the bigger tent to drop their animosities and check their egos. It's not about us, after all. It's about keeping watch on those in power, about ensuring an informed citizenry, about maintaining a democratic culture that is strengthened by vibrant reporting on vital institutions.

Traditional Journalistic Ethics Do Not Fit the Internet Well

Steve Smith

Steve Smith is a columnist for Media Industry Newsletter *(MIN) and a media consultant.*

As with anything on the vast internet, finding examples of egregious lapses in editorial judgment and traditional journalistic ethics is as brain-dead simple as a shallow Google search.

Journalistic Ethics on the Internet

To wit: In early September [2008], an investment reporter's Google search turns up a 2002 news story about United Airlines filing for bankruptcy, which he mistakenly reports as current news. When Bloomberg News Service links and pushes the erroneous story into countless investment houses, the company's stock tanks.

Also in September, a *Rocky Mountain News* reporter Twitters to a live blog the details of the high-profile funeral of a 3-year-old child killed by an ice cream truck. How invasive should always-on, always-there journalism be?

In 2006, Microsoft famously sent numerous independent bloggers free PCs [personal computers] loaded with its then-new Vista operating system. A firestorm ensued. Were tech companies detecting in the blogosphere a soft underbelly of digital journalism, in which traditional rules against accepting vendor gifts were unknown?

And, of course, libel and misinformation are everyday occurrences even in the comments sections of most branded media sites. How responsible is a content producer for the user-generated invective it hosts anyway?

This is a complex issue, to be sure. To take a spoon of traditional editorial medicine and approach the issue in an ethical way—which means talking to sources at the front lines of editorial quality in order to understand how (and how much) digital technology, distribution, business models, and democratized publishing have affected traditional notions of editorial integrity—well, suffice it to say, this process is a lot tougher than typing a few keywords into a search engine.

> *Most publishers and editors maintain that their ethics rules are the same online as in print, but digital technology makes it harder to control the online page.*

From a user perspective, the trustworthiness of this medium remains middling to good. The latest World Internet Project survey finds that 47% of U.S. internet users feel most information on the web is reliable, and 43% consider about half of it is trustworthy. The dozen or so content editors, publishers, and academics I consulted on these questions were generally more sanguine about the resiliency of editorial integrity online, but a number of flash points in recent years reveal an industry still trying to keep up with a new range of challenges. Egregious violations are less the issue than the unforeseen ways in which fuzzy ethics creep in at the borders.

Church and State: Advertising and Editorial

By its very nature, digital media brings advertising and editorial into a tighter relationship than print tolerates. Ad-targeting technologies such as Google AdWords and most display-ad networks routinely match ad messages with directly relevant copy. "Contextual advertising is very similar to something that the ASBPE [American Society of Business Publication Editors] does call a violation in print," says business media consultant

Paul Conley, "Placing ads against editorial implies a relationship to the advertising." However, readers online not only understand this difference but even prefer it, argues former editor of *PC World* Harry McCracken. "Based on what readers told us, it made their research easier to see an ad for an HP [Hewlett-Packard] PC next to a review of [the PC]."

Most publishers and editors maintain that their ethics rules are the same online as in print, but digital technology makes it harder to control the online page. In business publishing, a signature controversy over church and state in recent years surrounded "in-text" advertising, where keywords within editorial text are hyperlinked to a relevant advertiser. "That is a glaring example of a new style of violation where someone was selling material within the editorial well," says Conley, who crusaded against the practice for years. In 2004, *Forbes* editors forced the publication to end the practice, but the IntelliTXT product, sold to publishers by the Vibrant Media ad network, popped up again recently at Ziff-Davis and other sites.

Technology allows ads a closer proximity to directly relevant editorial, but that doesn't necessarily change the editorial principles behind it.

The ASBPE rules state that ad links in editorial can occur only at the discretion of the editors and when disclosed to the readers. Vibrant Media contends in its editorial policy statement that IntelliTXT links "cannot influence, or be influenced, by the editorial team," because the real-time, automated process occurs only after the editorial is produced. This is not good enough, says Jeffrey Seglin, ethics columnist for the *New York Times* Syndicate. "[The reader] doesn't know who is making the decision. Is it the technology?" Even worse, the technology may tempt editors to optimize their own copy in advance to include keywords that enhance "in-text" monetization.

It is not that old questions of church and state or editorial accuracy are new to the digital age. It is that "these kinds of problems have ballooned with the new technology," says Roy Harris, senior editor, CFO [chief financial officer], and former president of ASBPE, who serves on the organization's ethics committee. "It is a more undefined relationship. It is amazing the number and variety of challenges that arise," he says. Increasingly, business publication editors contact the organization for help or advice about the new opportunities for business and editorial interests to blur, so the ASBPE recently created a standing ethics committee to field such queries more rapidly.

Undoubtedly, online media models encourage new minglings.

Yes, technology allows ads a closer proximity to directly relevant editorial, but that doesn't necessarily change the editorial principles behind it. "Pat McGovern started this publication with pissing off advertisers as one of his goals," says *Computerworld* editor-in-chief Scot Finnie. "I don't think it changes. We are always exploring editorially in new media, but I don't have any trouble with the most obvious differences." What does concern Finnie is the way online platforms allow vendors to become publishers, and trade publications such as his do have white papers and vendor research on the same site as independent editorial. "It is easy if we are not careful for visitors to be confused," so labeling is especially important. In print, these distinctions were more obvious, but online, it is necessary to think it through. "That is where everyone is now," he says.

Old Bedfellows, New Models

Beyond the simple proximity of ads to content, new multi-platform business models can change the relationship between vendors and publishers. "There is a certain amount of experimentation that allows for some looser standards and less rigorous ethical practices," says Bob Steele, director [of] The Poynter Institute's ethics program. "How much should we borrow from the print side in our values and standards?" United Business Media's Everything Channel is an example of an evolving B2B business model in which a trade publisher also now offers workflow tools and consultations, including product sales help to its own advertisers. Nevertheless, CEO [chief executive officer] Robert Faletra insists, "The essence of integrity still holds true," and his editors and business people are kept wholly separate.

Undoubtedly, online media models encourage new minglings. Webinar and webcast formats sometimes blur a line that has been clearer with offline advertorial products, analysts contend. Many trade publishers offer custom webcasts that feature a sponsor's product but also include preambles from the staff editors. Faletra says he instructs editors that their portion of the show is independent of the sponsors', and they should say "what [they] believe and see in the market—*then* the vendor talks about their offering." But Seglin warns that online webcasting is different from the traditional third-party, live conference with editorial moderators. "When it is sponsored by the advertiser, then it becomes questionable who the editor is working for. Perception is everything. What message is this sending to the readers?" Harris concurs that sponsored webcasts involving editorial staff are fundamentally different from print advertorial. "In webcasts it gets more confused because the sponsorship seems more deeply integrated." Faletra counters that print traditions online are not quite apt. "It is a different medium that grew up in different ways," he says. He suggests that webcast models are less akin to print than to radio, where hosts often introduce advertisers.

Yet the real hobgoblins live in the new distributions models digital media introduced, says Larry Rafsky, CEO of Acquire Media, which aggregates thousands of feeds for institutions. He points to "bogus stock touts" as an insidious trap sprung on many content aggregators. Small companies will craft releases and false news stories that tie them deceptively to a story involving larger public companies. Search spiders and repackagers mistake these advertorial links as big company news, and they can quickly pollute an automated feed and link economy and can even show up in the feeds at major brokerage houses. "There are dozens of these a day," says Rafsky. "It is a cat-and-mouse game, and we do a very brisk business in keeping a list of bad actors."

The Issue of Accuracy

Celebrity rumors and premature claims of Steve Jobs' death aside, the internet has proven a remarkably accurate source of business and professional information, many in the industry contend. "It is surprising, in a way," says *BusinessWeek Online* editor-in-chief John Byrne. "You would expect a lot more unsubstantiated rumors that would affect companies or exacerbate crises. But [overall] that has not been the case." In Elsevier's scientific and medical journal business, digitization has only helped not hindered the peer-review process, says Philippe Terheggen, director, journal development and support. Editors can detect plagiarism and gauge originality faster and more accurately. "The transparency is better," he says. And yet, the self-publishing ethos of the web lowers the barrier of entry to beginning scientists. "We see a flooding of articles and paper submissions that don't have the right standard yet."

In fact, it is source-mingling, the new proximity of user, advertiser, and editorial voices on the same page, that keeps many editors up at night. Is a publication's brand at stake when its own scrupulously sourced content shares a page with user comments that include invective and innuendo? With dwindling staff to monitor ballooning user-generated content, editors increasingly rely on the community to flag bad actors.

Which raises another ethics issue: Should publishers be censoring readers, and, if so, when should they be censored? "We are learning it is complex," says Finnie. "It can give us tough afternoons." However, Steele worries about something worse: that editorial might start instigating online "mosh pits" in order to court traffic. "The main reason they have done this is not noble but to get eyeballs," he says. "The attempt to get feedback has resulted in the spewing of hatred."

The same democratized publishing platform that can lead to error also proves remarkably self-correcting.

Curiously, despite conventional wisdom about the unreliability of an unprofessional blogosphere, most editors share Rafsky's view that, "The real good news about the blogs is you know where you get them from." Acquire Media feeds carry thousands of blogs, and Rafsky has never needed to suppress them. In the financial sector especially, he says, "The blog universe, paradoxically, is actually a bit purer. Blogging tends to be more personal and doesn't cloak itself in the respectability of a review." In fact, publishers such as Computerworld, Inc. are networking many nonprofessional bloggers under their brand umbrella. Finnie has a staff "blog editor" with whom these 50 bloggers of varying journalistic backgrounds must check on editorial questions. "It is not as easy as it was in the old days when everyone was a pro," admits Finnie. But publishers must also embrace the voice and authenticity of the web's new forms by finding ways to police talented amateurs. He argues that the blogosphere actually has improved in recent years as bloggers become businesspeople and recognize that inaccuracy is bad for their bottom lines.

Conley goes further, suggesting that in the business information space, it is the endemic web-only publishers who view the traditional B2B [business-to-business] brands with suspicion because of their long-standing, integrated relationships with vendors. "A lot of us came out of the print world expecting untoward behavior in the web world, but my experience has been quite different. [Web-only publishers] see themselves taking advocacy positions and not pandering to advertisers . . . and main B2B magazines are less a journalistic look at an industry and more a part of the industry itself."

Crowd-sourced Integrity

Speed and diminished resources not only task reporters with monitoring integrity but readers as well. The same democratized publishing platform that can lead to error also proves remarkably self-correcting. Many editors agree with Seglin that in the professional content space especially, "There are more people watching other people and taking them to task when there are egregious lapses in judgment." Rafsky also reminds hand-wringing critics of the blogosphere that one original promise of digital aggregation was *increasing* editorial integrity—"the belief that mainstream media were excluding a lot of smaller voices that needed to be distributed. The point was to be ecumenical." The danger of overcorrecting for perceived lapses in a populist-content ecosystem is a "slippery slope" that returns to an oligarchy where old media alone are trusted media. His five editors vet content by aggregating the award-winning and trusted blogs but also by relying on references from his own clients. "It is the web trust model," he says. It is not surprising that new technology and business models invite new checks and balances, says Finnie. "We are in a period of incredibly rapid change where the quality rules still apply, but how we get to that quality has changed."

Yet this new multivocal, multimedia platform is taxing the pros too, with unexpected drags on quality. Impartial reporters are now online bloggers, videographers, and photographers. "If ever there was a recipe for disaster, that sure seems like it," says Steele. An obsession with always-on speed to market content creates mistakes that echo on the web long after we correct the original. "There are not nearly enough editors on the internet side to bring meaningful checks and balances," he says. "There is a terrible erosion of quality controls in the oversight process. We run faster and think less." McCracken agrees that the hunger for page views and the elimination of fact-checking creates an ecosystem that regards error too casually. "You will get the page view even if it turns out what you reported was not true," he says. Almost all editors agree that the absence of fact-checking in 24/7 publishing models creates a real shift in accountability where reporters, not editors, police integrity. Seglin says even on this rapid-response platform, "there needs to be some kind of filter . . . even a quick filter." Can integrity and reader trust in the editorial product really be crowd-sourced?

The big concern now is that any internal integrity filters and old church/state pieties will be the first to go as a deep media downturn combines with a historic recession. Almost all editors worry that the current crisis not only causes layoffs of many of the watchmen but also gives sponsors enormous leverage. As organizations cut content services such as Rafsky's, do they risk losing whatever quality filter the aggregated web has? "You think it is bad now—what happens when you disintermediate people like us that care about it," he says. Even the publishers who do continue to care may need to ask how much editorial integrity they can afford. Byrne warns that it "will put undue pressure on a lot of organizations to do things they would not have done. Now it comes down to survival. You are going to see things we haven't seen."

Social Networking Raises Ethical Issues for Journalists

Pamela J. Podger

Pamela J. Podger is an adjunct instructor at the University of Montana School of Journalism.

As a journalist, is it okay to describe your politics as "kind of a Commie" on Facebook?

Do you stop friends from posting pictures of you on their MySpace pages?

How about that video of you at the tailgate party going up on YouTube?

Ethics Guidelines for Social Networks

For journalists today, social networking sites are increasingly blurring the line between the personal and professional, creating a host of ethics and etiquette questions for news outlets.

In the past, Facebook, MySpace and LinkedIn were mined mainly for research and background, but these days more and more journalists are players in these cyber sandboxes. Age is no limit, with journalists in their 20s to their 90s exploring social networking tools.

News organizations—dealing with a flood of unedited, unfiltered remarks appearing digitally—are busily crafting ethics guidelines for the growing number of staffers using social networks. These documents aim to be malleable and adapt to changes in the new technology—be it using Twitter material from Iran with all the advantages and disadvantages of eyewitness tweets to hunting on Facebook for relatives and friends of a skier lost in the mountains.

Pamela J. Podger, "The Limits of Control: With Journalists and Their Employter Increasingly Active on Social Media Sites Like Facebook and Twitter, News Organizations Are Struggling to Respond to a Host of New Ethics Challenges," *American Journalism Review*, vol. 31, no. 4, August–September 2009, pp. 32–37. Copyright © 2009 by the American Journalism Review. All rights reserved. Reproduced by permission.

Traditional newspapers are eager to harness the power of social networks to find and distribute information, but they also want to do it in a way that fosters responsible use. The goals are to identify the tripwires of social networks, avoid any appearance of impropriety and ensure the information can't be used to impugn the integrity of their reporters, photographers and editors.

For journalists, transparency is one of the most important values.

In recent months [Summer 2009], the *Wall Street Journal*, *New York Times*, Associated Press [AP], *Roanoke Times* and others have hammered out ethics guidelines for social networking. These range from restrictive uses to common sense approaches. Other papers, including the *Seattle Times*, *Sacramento Bee*, *Baltimore Sun*, *San Francisco Chronicle* and Spokane's *Spokesman-Review*, are in the process of doing so.

Mary Hartney, director of audience engagement at the *Baltimore Sun*, says reporters, editors, managers and others will help shape the new guidelines. "The technology is changing, so I hope the ethics policy is a living document," says Hartney, who estimates about half the *Sun*'s newsroom actively uses social networks. "All of this stuff is changing very rapidly. So, anything you write down in an ethics policy or as a best practice is liable to change next week."

The Value of Transparency

On social networks, you should identify yourself as a journalist, tell recipients if you're using social networks in a professional capacity and remain mindful that people will regard you as a representative of your newsroom, says Kelly McBride, ethics group leader at the Poynter Institute.

"For journalists, transparency is one of the most important values," she says. "That doesn't mean you don't act as an individual, but there should be a caution gate if there's anything that might embarrass your newsroom."

Already, news managers have faced some unexpected behavior in connection with social networking, such as young staffers at the *New York Times* tweeting tidbits from an internal meeting where Executive Editor Bill Keller spoke of generating new revenue from the Web. "The older generation understood that these were internal meetings, but to the younger generation, who enjoy being wired in with the outside world, this was news and they wanted to share," says *Times* Standards Editor Craig Whitney, who estimates about 30 percent of the *Times* staff uses social networks. "No one was reprimanded. They didn't intend anything malicious nor did they tip off the competition, but it was behavior we hadn't expected."

Whitney says the paper responded by asking staffers to turn off their cell phones in meetings and managers now remind people when information is proprietary. "At Bill's next meeting," he says, staffers should "bear in mind this is a meeting for us."

Despite the progress that many newsrooms are making in addressing social networking ethics and etiquette, questions still abound.

The Evolving Guidelines

As journalism evolves, some old-school conventions remain intact: Don't march in protests, don't contribute to a political campaign, don't stick a political placard in your front lawn. But what are the online equivalents as journalists participate in discussions in the virtual public square?

Ken Chavez, assistant managing editor for interactive media at the *Sacramento Bee*, says his paper has nearly completed its guidelines for online ethics. "Our new rules will reinforce the idea that these are public spaces and what they are saying is not private and their cyber footprint can be seen," he says. "They need to act professionally and realize what they can and cannot do in terms of exposing a political bias or creating a perception of favoritism."

Kathy Best, managing editor of digital news and innovation at the *Seattle Times*, says the growing number of questions in the newsroom is encouraging the paper to come up with guidelines by the fall. When do reporters "friend" sources? Do they risk revealing them? What if a source wants to friend a reporter?

While the *Times* follows the conventions against deleting posts or putting up compromising photos, Best says she can give advice but doesn't have all the answers. "There are many ways you can get into an uncomfortable place," she says. "I completely understand the idea of transparency, and that's what we preach here. But at what point does transparency begin to erode journalistic credibility? You could argue, 'If I lean a particular way, it is valuable for people to know.' But if you're good at your job, you don't want anybody to read your story and discern what your political leanings are."

Best estimated 70 to 80 percent of the *Times* staffers—young and old—use social networks, and that the determining factor isn't age but privacy. "Some people are very private and don't want anything to do with this stuff," she says. "Others are very gregarious, embrace it and are comfortable. I don't want to be in a position where I force someone to reveal themselves on the World Wide Web with a Facebook page."

Practicing Restraint and Protecting Privacy

Despite the progress that many newsrooms are making in addressing social networking ethics and etiquette, questions still abound. While experts say friending your boss will keep you honest, how does one delicately unfriend a boss? Is it okay to celebrate President [Barack] Obama's victory or make other political statements in a status update on your Facebook profile?

Matt Chittum, data delivery editor and a reporter at the *Roanoke Times*, says he's excited about social networks but practices restraint.

Some journalists say their activities on social networks are akin to gathering with coworkers at a corner pub.

"All those quippy remarks that formerly would only be heard by the guy sitting next to you in the newsroom, well, suddenly you're now saying this to 400 friends—so you don't want to post something regrettable," Chittum says. "These places become your virtual front yard. But all of a sudden, your neighborhood is a lot bigger and is visible from a lot more places."

He advises journalists to educate themselves about privacy settings on the sites, but he still takes the precaution of self-policing his utterances before he hits the send key on Facebook. "I worry there are a lot of side doors that you're not really aware of, and people can see things you're doing who are 'friends of friends,'" Chittum says. "If you've decided to keep your pages as personal, then you're not getting the benefit of putting your personality out there. It can be humanizing, but if you're not careful, inevitably it can backfire. I guess I'm still old school and think all of this should be done with a good deal of thought."

Sharing Opinions Online

Some journalists say their activities on social networks are akin to gathering with coworkers at a corner pub. They say they freely express their views to their online community of friends, relatives and colleagues.

Michael Cabanatuan, who covered transportation at the *San Francisco Chronicle* for nearly a decade, holds this view. He says he joined Facebook about two years ago and initially used it to track down friends and relatives of a lost skier. He says he now uses Facebook personally more than professionally, but that he didn't think twice about his Election Day remarks on the site.

While nothing he posted was outrageous, he started his status updates for the evening by saying he was "hoping we've overcome." He also said he voted "the Right Way," and when a friend asked if he meant to the left, he wrote, "You're Right."

At 6:53 p.m., he was "anxiously awaiting election results." Later, he remarked, "I'm ticked about Prop. 8," which eliminated the rights of gay couples in California to marry, and finally, at 2:49 a.m. on November 5, he wrote he was "ready to go to bed and wake up to a brighter world."

Months later, he says he doesn't have any regrets about his comments.

"At that time, I didn't have any friends who were sources, managers or bosses. I don't think anything went over the line because I wasn't covering those races. The remarks were innocuous and no one could tell how I voted," he says. "The whole nature of social media, particularly Facebook and Twitter, is people are asking to be your friend. It is not saying, 'Can I connect with you to see what your biases are?' If you're sharing opinions with friends, it seems like Facebook is the electronic equivalent of sitting around drinking in a bar with friends."

With his recent shift to general assignment, Cabanatuan says he will be more cautious given the wider range of issues he will cover.

"Social media is about building community and not isolating groups from each other," he says. "I find myself joining in discussions of friends of friends, and that's part of the appeal. If I want to be more opinionated, I'll defriend some of my sources or figure out some way to wall them off."

The Professional Use of Social Media

Monica Guzman, 26, a news gatherer at seattlepi.com, says her tweets are open, reflect her personality and link to her stories.

Once, on her way to cover a fashion show, she asked her Twitter followers what she should wear and posted photos of three possible outfits. She also notifies her Twitter followers about weekly face-to-face conversations in different Seattle neighborhoods.

She says she enjoys the "stream," or real-time aspect, of Twitter that captures the thoughts, influences and information surrounding an event, especially in a wired city like Seattle. "Journalism is about listening," Guzman says, "so if you're not listening to people who are talking, then you're not doing your job."

She "never, ever, ever" unpublishes or deletes tweets without explaining why she is doing so, and often will retweet with the correct information. "Social media makes us confront that we're not superhuman and we don't have all the answers," she says.

But she always identifies herself as a journalist, is careful about how she expresses herself and is "kind of a stickler" about allowing her friends to post photos of her. "You should never assume you can control anything you put online," Guzman says.

Separating the Personal and Professional

But other reporters prefer to have separate personal and professional pages on social networks. One is for friends, family and classmates, while the other is for sources, bosses and coworkers.

Cheryl Rossi, 38, an arts and community news reporter at the *Vancouver Courier* in British Columbia, says she segregates her work and personal lives on two Facebook accounts. Now she doesn't have to think twice about who is receiving her "warnings of my PMS [premenstrual syndrome] days on my status updates."

She has a more casual picture of herself dancing at a friend's wedding on her personal site and a head shot on her professional page.

"It might be me being technologically superstitious, but it just seems wrong for all of my friends and professional links to be in one place," Rossi says.

Matt Stannard, 39, who covers the San Francisco Bay Area delegation in Congress for the *San Francisco Chronicle*, says he has two Twitter accounts.

He first used Twitter about six months ago, sending tweets during an immigration protest and alerting drivers to blocked roads. The updates were interesting to those affected or involved in the protest, but they wouldn't warrant a complete rewrite of a story for the newspaper's Web site, he says.

Stannard said he now uses Twitter as a news aggregator for his followers and bookmarks information he's reading about the congressional delegation.

As the digital dynamic unfolds . . . some journalists say the mainstream media's traditionally authoritative voice is a thing of the past.

He has a separate personal Twitter account and would prefer that his followers recognize the distinction.

"My hope is people who're interested in what the Bay Area congressional delegation is up to will come to see me as a useful aggregator of that news," he says. "But I'm sufficiently old school that I like the idea that people can rely on a journalist to see what's going on and not have to wade through my opinions or what I think about something."

Hal Straus, assistant managing editor for interactivity and communities at the *Washington Post*, says his paper requires its reporters who use social networks to include their proper identity and clearly state what jobs they hold at the paper. "We want people to identify themselves online, period," he says. "Everything is provisional and platforms change, but we would be concerned by people having two pages—a public and a private page. Who are you on one page and who on another? Remember, we're in the most political place in America, and we try to report what all sides say and cannot be highly partisan. The *Post* is real clear about reporters not engaging in political speech."

Connecting with Communities

As the digital dynamic unfolds—rapidly, chaotically and in directions difficult to predict—some journalists say the mainstream media's traditionally authoritative voice is a thing of the past. News consumers want more insight into how news organizations and individual journalists operate; they want a glimpse of the human news gatherer, with all his foibles. In short, the public—once reliant on major news organizations to decide what's news—is demanding a seat at the newsmaking table.

Today's Internet readers have a 24/7 appetite for news, information and gossip—regardless of who produces it—and social networks can provide those heightened connections with their communities. For example, says Poynter's McBride, *New York Times* columnist Nicholas Kristof does a fine job integrating his Facebook presence with personal and professional tidbits, asking people questions and adding small amounts of analysis.

Amy Gahran, a consultant for the Knight Digital Media Center, says the best practices for journalists in social media include being personal, clever, edgy, receptive, grateful. Their goal is engaging the community, forging connections and creating a sense of belonging by asking questions, posting links, cultivating real-time debate and providing a place for instant, impressionistic feedback.

She adds, "Social media is one of the best ways to get traction with the mobile market. Far more people have crappy cell phones than computers. This allows journalists to reach lower and even middle-income communities and minorities that news organizations have been overlooking. Why are you a journalist in the first place?—hopefully it's more than writing articles and seeing your byline. It's to reach communities where they are, and they're on the phone."

Giving journalists the breathing room to connect candidly with people in their communities and show they participate in life is an upside of social networks, says Yoko Kuramoto-Eidsmoe, a copy editor and page designer at the *Seattle Times*. She says she's very open about her personal views, describing her politics as "kind of a Commie" on Facebook.

"Maybe it's making people more comfortable with the idea that a journalist is a complete person, that you don't exempt yourself from other facets of life," she says. "The mid-20th century concept of what a journalist is and the whole objectivity doctrine kind of assumes that you don't live and participate in the world. I hope social media is changing this."

A Variety of Approaches to Ethics

So how do traditional news organizations write guidelines that allow a relaxed, casual interaction with readers while maintaining standards such as accuracy, fairness, context and verification? Each news outlet's culture seems to define its approach.

Staffers are always representing the *Los Angeles Times* [*LAT*] in online activities, according to the paper's guidelines on social media. "Assume that your professional life and your personal life merge online regardless of your care in separating them. Don't write or post anything that would embarrass the *LAT* or compromise your ability to do your job."

At the *Wall Street Journal*, staffers are advised not to mix "business and pleasure" in their postings. They are told not to "recruit friends or family to promote or defend your work." And "sharing your personal opinions, as well as expressing partisan political views, whether on Dow Jones sites or on the larger Web, could open us up to criticism that we have biases and could make a reporter ineligible to cover topics in the future for Dow Jones."

The AP guidelines say the wire service has a "robust corps of employees" with accounts on various social networks. The organization says comments on staffers' Facebook pages should meet AP guidelines. "It's a good idea to monitor your profile page to make sure material posted by others doesn't violate AP standards; any such material should be deleted."

Regarding Twitter, "We're still the AP. Don't report things or break news that we haven't published, no matter the format, and that includes retweeting unconfirmed things not fit for AP's wires."

As journalists' use of social media evolves, there are likely to be continued ripples in the workplace.

Tony Winton, an AP reporter and the president of the News Media Guild representing about 1,100 AP editorial staffers across the country, says the union is reviewing the policy with legal counsel and has concerns it is "overly broad." "These guidelines have a chilling effect on proper, ordinary conversation that people have with their coworkers," Winton says. "Facebook is an explosive social networking tool of today and tomorrow. We believe you have a right to interact with your coworkers about things in the news industry. It is a protected area of speech."

Issues Beyond Social Networks

Amy Webb, principal consultant at Webbmedia Group in Baltimore, says news organizations are late with "their edicts, ethics and codes" about social networks. Instead, they should be pondering the privacy and safety issues of a new crop of tools, including location-aware services.

"When a *New York Times* reporter logs on to Facebook from his mobile phone, he's sharing a lot more information than his status updates. He's sharing the content he wrote and his location," Webb says. "There are safety and privacy issues around this."

As journalists' use of social media evolves, there are likely to be continued ripples in the workplace. "Transparency, accuracy and minimizing harm carry over to social media, and there will be a continuing conversation on how best to do this," Seattlepi.com's Guzman says. "The technology will always be changing, and we need to be mindful that there will be new ways to screw up."

The Growth in News Websites Necessitates Clear Policies on Removing Stories

Andrew Alexander

Andrew Alexander is a Scripps Howard Visiting Professional at Ohio University E.W. Scripps School of Journalism and former ombudsman for The Washington Post.

Nearly 23 years ago, *The Post*'s Metro section reported that Joseph P. Unice, a chief deputy for the U.S. Marshals Service, had been charged with indecent exposure at a Woodbridge McDonald's. But *The Post* never reported what happened next.

Requests for "Unpublishing"

According to Unice, a judge quickly concluded that the incident had been inadvertent and the case went no further. As he recounted it last week [August 2010], he'd forgotten to wear an athletic supporter while running and his gym shorts were too revealing for several patrons at the McDonald's where he stopped afterward. "It wasn't intentional," Unice said.

He hired an attorney and got the charges expunged, so there is no public record, he said. His career with the U.S. Marshals Service continued until he retired in 2003. "I just let it go," said Unice, now 65 and living in the western Ohio community of Miamisburg.

But last year [2009], when he started looking for jobs to supplement his retirement income, Unice said prospective employers Googled his name and found the two brief stories *The Post* had written in 1987—not on *The Post*'s Web site but on research Web sites that archive *Post* stories. "They won't hire me," he said. "I never realized that 23 years later it would come back to haunt me."

He wants the stories to disappear. Google says that removing news stories is up to the Web site that published them. That's why Unice contacted *The Post*. "I'm really in need of your help," he pleaded, noting that he can't point employers to court records because they were expunged.

A growing number of requests to unpublish are like the one from Unice, where the issue is fairness.

News Web sites such as *The Post*'s increasingly hear from people who want information "unpublished." In rare instances, requests are granted. For example, *The Post* deleted a woman's name as the purchaser of a home because she feared being located by a stalker.

Most requests are simply efforts to avoid embarrassment. Occasionally it's so-called "source remorse," when someone *The Post* quoted wants to revise their comments to make them more articulate. Or it's a request to remove a news brief about a drunken driving conviction.

The Post properly rejects these. Altering a newspaper's historical record, which lives in digital databases and is relied on for research, can erode credibility.

But a growing number of requests to unpublish are like the one from Unice, where the issue is fairness.

A Lack of Guidelines

"What's surprising is how few news organizations have policies to deal with things like this," said Mallary Jean Tenore, who has examined the issue for the Poynter Institute on media studies in Florida.

The Post has no written policies. Requests are handled ad hoc throughout the newsroom, with some referred to *Post* attorneys. They are not tracked, so *The Post* has no firm grasp on the volume or types of requests being made. And readers are left in the dark about *The Post*'s rules on unpublishing or even how they might submit a request.

A brief reference to unpublishing is included in a draft of updated corrections guidelines that is being reviewed by top *Post* editors. It reads: "We generally won't 'unpublish' or simply remove articles or blog posts after discovering an error. We can republish a corrected version as soon as possible, with the acknowledgement of the original error."

Senior Editor Milton Coleman, who helped develop the guidelines, said that when dealing with requests to unpublish, "Our general approach has been to say that something that occurred was fact, we reported it and we cannot and should not act like it did not occur. But since these things live forever online, we can correct the record online, and that is what we will do."

That makes sense. But what about cases where the material is accurate but incomplete? What of situations where *The Post* reported the charge, but not the dismissal of it? What about fairness to those who were accused but later vindicated?

Alternatives to "Unpublishing"

The Post's guidelines for these situations should make clear not only which types of unpublishing requests should be granted but also the range of remedies. When is it best to order a follow-up story that links to the original one? Is it permissible to simply post an "update" atop an archived online story, noting later developments? And what is the level of proof that is required from people like Unice in order to convince *The Post* that a criminal charge went away?

All of these guidelines for unpublishing should be spelled out to the newsroom. But just as important, they should be explained to readers on *The Post*'s Web site. Readers appreciate transparency, which builds loyalty and trust.

Organizations to Contact

The editors have compiled the following list of organizations concerned with the issues debated in this book. The descriptions are derived from materials provided by the organizations. All have publications or information available for interested readers. The list was compiled on the date of publication of the present volume; the information provided here may change. Be aware that many organizations take several weeks or longer to respond to inquiries, so allow as much time as possible.

Accuracy in Media (AIM)
4455 Connecticut Ave. NW, Suite 330, Washington, DC   20008
(202) 364-4401 • fax: (202) 364-4098
e-mail: info@aim.org
website: www.aim.org

AIM is a conservative watchdog group that criticizes liberal bias in the media. The group monitors the news media for biased or inaccurate stories and publishes critiques of these stories. These critiques can be found in AIM's twice-monthly newsletter; in its syndicated weekly newspaper column; and in reports, briefings, and columns that appear on AIM's website.

Center for International Media Ethics (CIME)
9215 South Pulaski Rd., Suite 1N, Evergreen Park, IL   60805
e-mail: info@cimethics.org
website: www.cimethics.org

CIME is a nonprofit, international organization that encourages journalists to formulate and enforce a code of ethics within the profession. CIME aims to bring together a network of journalists throughout the world to provide training, discussion, and expertise on ethics. Publications available at CIME's website include "Media Ethics Survey 2011" and its monthly newsletters.

Center for Journalism Ethics

School of Journalism and Mass Communication
University of Wisconsin-Madison, 5152 Vilas Hall
821 University Ave., Madison, WI   53706
e-mail: ethics@journalism.wisc.edu
website: http://ethics.journalism.wisc.edu

The Center for Journalism Ethics aims to advance the ethical standards and practices of democratic journalism. Through its website, the Center for Journalism Ethics aims to be a source for analyzing ethics issues. The organization publishes news, book reviews, interviews, the monthly *Ethical Connections* newsletter, and the blog *Media Morals.*

Center for Media Literacy (CML)

22631 Pacific Coast Highway #472, Malibu, CA   90265
(310) 804-3985
website: www.medialit.org

CML promotes media literacy—the ability to communicate competently in all media forms as well as to access, understand, analyze, evaluate, and participate in contemporary mass media culture. CML promotes the teaching of media literacy in schools through advocacy and teacher training. The organization publishes *CONNECTIONS*, a monthly newsletter for teachers, parents, administrators, and policy makers, available at its website.

Committee of Concerned Journalists (CCJ)

Donald W. Reynolds Journalism Institute
Administrative Offices, Suite 300, Columbia, MO   65211
(573) 884-9121 • fax: (573) 884-3824
e-mail: wdean@concernedjournalists.org
website: www.rjionline.org/ccj

CCJ works to strengthen journalism's future by advocating for the core principles and functions of journalism. Although it ceased to exist as an operating organization on December 31, 2011, the work and legacy of CCJ and its members continues through a variety of means, including in cooperation with the Donald W. Reynolds Journalism Institute through the books and ideas the group inspired, and with the Project for Excellence in Journalism. Its publications include the book *The Elements of Journalism: What Newspeople Should Know and the Public Should Expect*; *BLUR: How to Know What's True in the Age of Information Overload*; and a collection of tools for journalists, students, and citizens, which are available on the CCJ Section of the Reynolds Institute website. Commentary, research, speeches, and a Verification Application are also available.

Donald W. Reynolds Journalism Institute (RJI)
Administrative Offices, Suite 300, Columbia, MO   65211
(573) 884-9121 • fax: (573) 884-3824
e-mail: rji@rjionline.org
website: www.rjionline.org

RJI exists to develop and test ways to improve journalism through new technology and improved processes. RJI engages media professionals, scholars, and other citizens in programs aimed at improving the practice and understanding of journalism in democratic societies. The institute also posts news and commentary at its website and has a large collection of press codes of ethics available to view.

Fairness & Accuracy in Reporting (FAIR)
104 W. 27th St., Suite 10B, New York, NY   10001
(212) 633-6700 • fax: (212) 727-7668
e-mail: fair@fair.org
website: www.fair.org

FAIR is a national media watchdog group that advocates for greater diversity in the press, offering criticism of media bias and censorship. FAIR scrutinizes media practices that marginalize public interest, minority, and dissenting viewpoints and, as an anti-censorship organization, aims to expose neglected news stories and defend working journalists when they are muzzled. FAIR publishes the magazine *Extra!*, produces the weekly radio program *CounterSpin*, and publishes studies and reports.

Media Matters for America
PO Box 52155, Washington, DC   20091
(202) 756-4100
website: http://mediamatters.org

Media Matters for America is a nonprofit, progressive research and information center dedicated to monitoring, analyzing, and correcting conservative misinformation in the US media. Media Matters works daily to notify activists, journalists, pundits, and the general public about instances of misinformation. Media Matters publishes research and reports, documenting what it sees as conservative misinformation throughout the media.

Media Research Center (MRC)
325 S. Patrick St., Alexandria, VA   22314
(703) 683-9733 • fax: (703) 683-9736
e-mail: mrc@mrc.org
website: www.mrc.org

MRC is a nonprofit organization whose mission is to educate the public and media on bias in the media. MRC seeks to bring balance to the news media. The group publishes research and reports, documenting what it sees as liberal bias in the media.

The Poynter Institute
801 3rd St. S, St. Petersburg, FL   33701
(727) 821-9494
e-mail: webstaff@poynter.org
website: www.poynter.org

The Poynter Institute is a school dedicated to teaching and inspiring journalists and media leaders. The Institute teaches journalists, teachers, students, and the general public through seminars, newsrooms, and online podcasts and tutorials. The Poynter Institute publishes news and reports at its website, including in its *Everyday Ethics* blog.

Project for Excellence in Journalism (PEJ)

1615 L St. NW, Suite 700, Washington, DC   20036
(202) 419-3650 • fax: (202) 419-3699
e-mail: mail@journalism.org
website: www.journalism.org

PEJ, a project of the nonpartisan Pew Research Center, is dedicated to trying to understand the information revolution. PEJ uses empirical methods to evaluate and study the performance of the press, particularly content analysis. The organization publishes the annual *State of the News Media*, a report on the health and status of American journalism.

Radio Television Digital News Association (RTDNA)

529 14th St. NW, Suite 425, Washington, DC   20045
(800) 807-8632 • fax: (202) 223-4007
website: www.rtdna.org

RTDNA is the world's largest professional organization exclusively serving the electronic news profession. The association is dedicated to setting standards for newsgathering and reporting through publications, training, advocacy, and networking. At its website, RTDNA has information on ethics and other best practices, such as "Guidelines for Avoiding Conflict of Interest."

Reporters Committee for Freedom of the Press

1101 Wilson Blvd., Suite 1100, Arlington, VA   22209
(703) 807-2100
website: www.rcfp.org

Reporters Committee for Freedom of the Press was founded in 1970 to help journalists fight subpoenas that would require them to disclose their confidential sources. The committee maintains a hotline for journalists needing legal advice and advocates in legal cases related to the freedom of the press. It publishes the quarterly magazine, *The News Media & The Law*, as well as a number of pamphlets and handbooks that catalog the laws protecting journalists.

Society of Professional Journalists (SPJ)
Eugene S. Pulliam National Journalism Center
3909 N. Meridian St., Indianapolis, IN   46208
(317) 927-8000 • fax: (317) 920-4789
website: www.spj.org

SPJ is dedicated to the perpetuation of a free press as the cornerstone of the nation and of liberty. The organization works to protect the First Amendment guarantees of freedom of speech and of the press while stimulating ethical behavior in the practice of journalism. SPJ publishes a blog on ethics, *Code Words*, the magazine *Quill*, and a code of ethics that is voluntarily followed by members of the profession.

Bibliography

Books

David E. Boeyink and Sandra L. Borden
Making Hard Choices in Journalism Ethics: Cases and Practice. New York: Routledge, 2010.

Sandra L. Borden
Journalism as Practice: MacIntyre, Virtue Ethics, and the Press. New York: Routledge, 2009.

Fred Brown
Journalism Ethics: A Casebook of Professional Conduct for News Media. Portland, OR: Marion Street Press, 2011.

Michael J. Bugeja
Living Ethics: Across Media Platforms. New York: Oxford University Press, 2007.

Bruce E. Drushel and Kathleen German
Ethics of Emerging Media: Information, Social Norms, and New Media Technology. New York: Continuum, 2011.

Gene Foreman
The Ethical Journalist. Indianapolis, IN: Wiley-Blackwell, 2009.

Cecilia Friend and Jane B. Singer
Online Journalism Ethics: Traditions and Transitions. Armonk, NY: M.E. Sharpe, 2007.

Tom Goldstein
Journalism and Truth: Strange Bedfellows. Evanston, IL: Northwestern University Press, 2007.

Neil Henry   *American Carnival: Journalism Under Siege in an Age of New Media.* Berkeley: University of California Press, 2007.

Christopher Meyers   *Journalism Ethics: A Philosophical Approach.* New York: Oxford University Press, 2010.

Philippe Perebinossoff   *Real-World Media Ethics: Inside the Broadcast and Entertainment Industries.* Boston: Elsevier, 2008.

Patrick Lee Plaisance   *Media Ethics: Key Principles for Responsible Practice.* Los Angeles: Sage Publications, 2008.

Jason M. Shepard   *Privileging the Press: Confidential Sources, Journalism Ethics, and the First Amendment.* El Paso, TX: LFB Scholarly Publishing, 2011.

Ron F. Smith   *Ethics in Journalism.* Indianapolis, IN: Wiley-Blackwell, 2008.

Stephen J. A. Ward   *Ethics and the Media: An Introduction.* New York: Cambridge University Press, 2011.

Periodicals and Internet Sources

Mark Bowden   "The Story Behind the Story," *Atlantic*, October 2009.

Robert S. Boynton   "Checkbook Journalism Revisited: Sometimes We Owe Our Sources Everything," *Columbia Journalism Review*, January–February 2008.

Mark A. Grannis   "Justice and the Press," *Wall Street Journal*, March 15, 2008.

Austen Ivereigh   "An Unexpected Lesson in Media Ethics," *America*, July 13, 2011. www.americamagazine.org.

Gary Kamiya   "The Death of News," *Salon*, February 17, 2009. www.salon.com.

Howard Kurtz   "British Tabloid Tactics Are Rampant in American Journalism, Too," *Washington Post*, July 10, 2011.

John Lanchester   "Riots, Terrorism etc.," *London Review of Books*, March 6, 2008.

Nicholas Lemann   "Bad Press," *New Yorker*, August 1, 2011.

Mark Lisheron   "Lying to Get the Truth," *American Journalism Review*, October–November 2007.

Kelly McBride   "Journalists Must Expose, Not Perpetuate, Bogus News," *Poynter*, September 2, 2009. www.poynter.org.

Andrew C. McCarthy   "The *Los Angeles Times*'s Strange Notion of Journalistic Ethics," *National Review Online*, October 30, 2008. www.nationalreview.com.

Martha T. Moore   "NPR Sting Raises Questions About Media Ethics, Influence," *USA Today*, March 17, 2011.

John Morton — "Too Steep a Price: Newspapers Must Protect Their Integrity as They Struggle to Find New Revenue Streams," *American Journalism Review*, August–September 2009.

Robert Niles — "Online, News Archives Never Die, Nor Do They Fade Away," *OJR: The Online Journalism Review*, July 13, 2010. www.ojr.org.

Raymond T. Odierno — "The Photograph of a Dying Soldier," *New York Times*, February 3, 2007.

David Paulin — "*Boston Globe* Outs Whitey Bulger's FBI Tipster," *American Thinker*, October 10, 2011. www.americanthinker.com.

Leonard Pitts — "'Citizen Journalism' Fad Is Not Journalism," *Chicago Tribune*, October 6, 2010.

Rem Rieder — "Reporting to Conclusions: Journalists Shouldn't Shrink from Making Judgments About Factual Disputes," *American Journalism Review*, February 16, 2011.

Gabriel Schoenfeld — "Can the U.S. Bring Assange to Justice?" *Wall Street Journal*, December 8, 2010.

Jacob Sullum — "Is Julian Assange a Journalist? For First Amendment Purposes, It Doesn't Matter," *Reason*, April 2011.

Esther Thorson and Michael R. Fancher	"The Public and Journalists: They Disagree on Core Values," Nieman Reports, Fall 2009. www.nieman.harvard.edu.
Juan Williams	"Juan Williams: I Was Fired for Telling the Truth," FoxNews.com, October 21, 2010. www.foxnews.com.
Allan Wolper	"Trial by Media: Headlines Declare Guilt Before Juries Do," *Editor & Publisher*, October 2011.

Index

A

ABC's PrimeTime Live (TV show), 58–59

Abu Ghraib prison, 71

Accuracy
    by candidates, 36, 64, 114
    commitment to, 153, 172
    importance of, 143
    issues of, 159–161
    of journalists, 92, 100, 119, 121, 139, 141
    of new technology, 174, 177
    by news sources, 28
    of news stories, 18–19, 21–26, 59, 122, 125
    in online reporting, 159–162
    of press predictions, 104
    truth and, 69

Acquire Media, 158–160

Ad hominem (personal attack), 73

Advertising ethics
    benefits of, 45
    church and state in, 155–157
    conflict of, 47
    debate over, 44–45
    need for, 43–45
    overview, 43–44

Al Qaeda terrorists, 73, 75

Albom, Mitch, 39

Alexander, Andrew, 175–177

Allen, Mike, 105

Alterman, Eric, 116

American Advertising Federation, 44

American Journalism Review (magazine), 80, 118

American Society of Business Publication Editors (ASBPE), 155–157

Andrews, Caesar, 116

Anonymity promises, 48, 77

APCO lobbying firm, 54–55

Armey, Dick, 68

Assange, Julian, 51–52, 75–78

Associated Press (AP) guidelines, 173

Association of Community Organizations for Reform Now (ACORN), 82–83

Auletta, Ken, 70

Axe, David, 128–131

B

Baltimore Sun (newspaper), 39, 164

BankAtlantic Financial, 59

Baron, Martin, 92, 95

Bay Area Air Quality Management District, 111

Bernstein, Carl, 15–16

Best, Kathy, 166

BigGovernment.com (website), 79

Blackston, Michelle, 148

Blogs/blogging
    credentialing with, 147
    ethics of, 137–140, 145
    impact of, 91–95
    impartiality of, 98
    journalism *vs.*, 145–146, 149–150
    leaked materials on, 52
    manipulation by, 86–87
    objectivity on, 128

N